# You're Not My Friend Anymore!

# You're Not My Friend Anymore!

## Illustrated Answers to Questions About Young Children's Challenging Behaviors

By Betsy Evans
Illustrated by Jonathan Wilcox

HighScope®

*Published by*
**HighScope® Press**
A division of the HighScope Educational Research Foundation
600 North River Street
Ypsilanti, Michigan 48198-2898
734.485.2000, Fax: 734.485.0704
press@highscope.org
www.highscope.org



**Editor:** Joanne Tangorra, HighScope Press
**Book Design:** Margaret FitzGerald
**Cover Design:** Kazuko Sacks and Jonathan Wilcox
**Design and Production:** Kazuko Sacks, Profit Makers LLC
**Photos:** Betsy Evans: 90, 91
Gregory Fox: 1, 93
HighScope Staff: 2, 4

**Library of Congress Cataloging-in-Publication Data**
Evans, Betsy.
"You're not my friend anymore!" : illustrated answers to questions about young children's challenging behaviors / Betsy Evans.
p. cm.
Includes bibliographical references.
ISBN 978-1-57379-455-8 (soft cover : alk. paper) 1. Interpersonal conflict in children. 2. Interpersonal relations in children. 3. Adjustment (Psychology) in children. 4. Child rearing. I. Title.
BF723.I645E935 2009
649'.123--dc22

2009036011

Printed in the United States of America
10 9 8 7 6 5 4 3

*This book is dedicated to*

*my granddaughters,*

*Zoe, Sage, and Phoebe.*

# Contents

# Acknowledgments

*You're Not My Friend Anymore!* was motivated by a desire to make learning about problem-solving strategies more accessible and fun for those who are engaged in busy, possibly stressful lives. To construct an illustrated book such as this required a lot of discussion and feedback from friends and colleagues, parents, and teachers — all of whom encouraged me along the way. They are my personal version of the village that sustains me, but more importantly, they are my resources.

There are many people who participated, directly and indirectly, in the long process of weaving words and images into a coherent book. First, Jon Wilcox, the illustrator, has made an enormous contribution to the book by capturing the spirit and energy of young children and the complex array of emotions that they express. It was not an easy task to transform my stick people drawings into characters that came alive on the page. Thank you, Jon, for your artistry and your patience throughout this process. I am also very grateful to my editor, Joanne Tangorra, whose insights, sense of humor, and organized attention to detail have helped me manage the complexity of this book. Thanks also to Nancy Brickman, director of publications, for her editorial vision and guidance; Katie Bruckner, publications assistant, for her careful preparation of the manuscript; and Margaret Fitzgerald and Kazuko Sacks for the design of this book.

The true stories illustrated in this book are from all over this country as well as the UK, and there are parents and teachers to thank for that. My British friend and colleague, Rachael Underwood, has contributed three stories as well as her time and expertise to the text and illustrations. Thanks also go to her children, Kate and Stan, who contributed by being in the stories and solving problems so creatively. Many thanks also to Josh Abrahams who contributed an inspiring story, reaffirming once again that children can negotiate vigorously *and* constructively. I am also grateful to him for his suggestions for the text and illustrations. As a young inner-city teacher, Josh has become a dedicated mediator and exceptional role model in his work with young children who are experiencing challenges.

I also want to thank Deborah Bazer, Viviane Black, Fay McComb, Odelle Kinder-Wells, and all the children of the Giving Tree School for their stories as well as the welcome they gave me whenever I came to play. One Giving Tree child in particular, Abby Leaf, taught us all that young children can become remarkable mediators and role models at a very young age. We will miss her dearly as she heads off to kindergarten. Thanks also to Jan Dowling and Terri Mitchell, for their stories and expertise on children with special needs. Thank you, Amy Mae Silva, for your story and inspired toddler mediations. A rousing thanks to Lisa Kovalsi, who can turn even the most grueling trip into a pleasant and affordable adventure.

Along with the readers already named (Rachael Underwood and Josh Abrahams), I also want to thank Rebecca Clemente, Melissa Kaden, Eveline MacDougall, and Joanne Breeze Norris for reflecting on the illustrations and text from their perspective as young parents and seasoned educators. Their comments helped me to be realistic about the intensely emotional challenges of being present to the needs and feelings of young children. Thanks also to Ann Epstein for bringing her expertise in early childhood development to the book's discussion of those issues.

A warm thank you to Cheryl Fox of the Mediation and Training Collaborative who taught me so much in the beginning of my mediation journey. Her calm, knowledgeable, and upbeat style was a gift.

This past year I spent many weeks with HighScope Training of Trainers (TOT) and Preschool Curriculum Course (PCC) groups in Ypsilanti, Michigan and Greenville, South Carolina. I received enthusiastic support from them for the problem-solving approach and the powerful impact it is having on the children in their classrooms. A hearty thanks to all of you.

I am also very grateful to my sons, Tryfan and Sorrel, and my sister, Patricia, who are always there when I need them. Along with friends and neighbors Barb Watson, Al Wallace, Sue Kramer, and Tony Mathews, they all show me regularly how to have a laugh and maintain a strong spirit even in the face of serious challenges.

Since this book is dedicated to my granddaughters, Zoe, Sage, and Phoebe, I want to acknowledge Heather and Devon, their parents, who do the hard, fun, and constant work of guiding them every day. It is easy for me to tell the story of one conflict and a bit of success as Zoe and Sage solve a problem, but Zoe and Sage's early success is the result of having parents who are always there for the full complexity of challenges that their children hand them daily. I have great admiration and respect for Heather, Devon, and all parents who remain present and continually thoughtful about what is best for their children.

I continue to be moved and inspired by my six-year-old granddaughter, articulate and energetic Zoe, who sparks imaginative fun for all of our family. And thanks to two-year-old Sage, who reminded me one day that while *understanding* the problems of a two-year-old can remain elusive, finding solutions can sometimes be remarkably easy. When I asked how she wanted to solve a problem I did not understand, she said simply, *hug*. And to baby Phoebe — we can see already that you have a strong, alert spirit. I'm looking forward to how you will surprise us and what we will learn about you, and ourselves, as you grow and develop.

And finally, special thanks go to my husband, Jeff, who generously puts up with the frequent absences and irregularity that my work brings to our life and home. His constant encouragement and belief in my work has been the solid road beneath my feet these 33 years.

# Introduction

As a young parent, and later as a young teacher, I often wished that children came with a troubleshooting manual. Cars do. Even my coffeemaker and answering machine did. Why not children? Sure, there is a wealth of how-to books on childrearing for parents (not to mention plenty of unsolicited advice from friends and family), and teachers are required to have training and practice before they become full-fledged educators in the classroom. Still, there is an assumption that parents and teachers have a "natural" ability to care for and work with children. Somehow, they are expected to *instinctively* know what to do where children are concerned. The truth is, we all need to think, feel, and reflect every day on our reactions and interactions with children. I now have three grandchildren, and I still delight in the experience of reflecting on problem-solving and learning along with them, as well with as the children in my school.

*You're Not My Friend Anymore!: Illustrated Answers to Questions About Young Children's Challenging Behaviors* is a way of sharing what I continue to learn from children. My first book, *You Can't Come to My Birthday Party!: Conflict Resolution with Young Children,* focuses on six problem-solving steps, which are detailed in 50 true stories of actual conflict-resolution situations and discussed in depth throughout the book. This second book looks even more closely and concretely at children's challenging behaviors and effective adult responses to those behaviors. While it is important to understand the theory and motives behind adult interactions with children, many parents and teachers want to know more specifically, *What if my child does…? What should I do and say?* The focus of this book is an exploration of some of those *What if…?* questions, shedding new light — through illustrated answers — on a simple and positive approach to children's problematic actions and words. *You're Not My Friend Anymore!* is a guide for parents and teachers as they reflect on their relationships and their goals for young children and what they can do and say to be consistent with those goals.

*As parents and teachers know, everyday conflicts are common among young children. Learning the skills to negotiate these conflicts is at the core of children's social and emotional growth.*

## What If…?

Since I began training in 1989, I have provided hundreds of trainings for parents and teachers in the United States and other countries, and I have been asked many *What if…?* questions. As students of problem solving, these adults have practiced, reflected, and sought out more information about the conflict situations they've encountered in their interactions with children. As these adults have continued to practice problem-solving strategies, they've experienced interesting and rewarding child-made solutions. Many of them have shared their stories (providing true stories for the situations illustrated in this book), while also generating more questions. And so it is with learning that new ideas and new experiences lead the way to more questions and even

## The Problem-Solving Steps

1. Approach calmly, stopping any hurtful actions.
2. Acknowledge children's feelings.
3. Gather information.
4. Restate the problem.
5. Ask for ideas for solutions and choose one together.
6. Be prepared to give follow-up support.

richer learning opportunities. I often end my training sessions with this final statement of encouragement: *See past the conflict to the opportunity.*

The six problem-solving steps are a set of tools for interacting with children during conflict situations. As parents and preschool teachers know, there is no shortage of these situations among children. Such negotiations are at the core of social-emotional growth and learning; they are necessary conversations that assist children as they learn to understand the diverse needs of others, what works in relationships, and how to express their own needs and wants. When adults regard conflicts with this in mind, it becomes easier to generate the energy and resolve that it takes to fully engage in and learn from a problem-solving discussion with children.

The six problem-solving strategies describe how to approach children calmly, how to acknowledge their feelings fully, how to understand a problem and repeat it back to the children, and how to support children's solutions. Knowing that there is so much to be learned, by the adults as well as the children, adults will find the patience to wait as they ask children, *What do you think we can do to solve this problem?* The result is the reward of child-made solutions, enriched relationships, and the growth of children's social-emotional competence.

*Using HighScope's problem-solving steps during conflict situations, teachers and parents respond to children by acknowledging and naming their feelings, understanding and restating the problem, and supporting child-made solutions.*

### About This Book

Each chapter in this book starts with a specific *What If…?* scenario and question, followed by a four-panel illustration of a "typical" situation and response to the problem or conflict situation described. Several aspects of these "typical" responses are discussed in the text, encouraging adults to reflect on their own interactions with children. One section explores the question *What Happened Here?* with a discussion of the problem situation, the factors that led to children's challenging behaviors, and the effect of the adult's "typical" response on the outcome of the situation. Another section *(Instead of... Try This...)* offers a comparative list of "typical" adult responses to children's challenging behaviors and alternative "problem-solving" strategies. Each chapter also includes a discussion entitled *What is the Reason...?* answering a common question related to a particular strategy or some aspect of a child's behavior.

A second illustration, drawn with six panels, describes a problem-solving response to the same *What If...?* question. This is followed by four sections of discussion. First, *What Happened Differently?* describes the adult's problem-solving approach to the situation and how the children involved responded. The next section, *Something More to Consider,* expands on a specific aspect of the situation or an issue related to it. For example, this section might explore further the reasons for using a particular problem-solving strategy or discuss in depth the kinds of skills children learn during problem-solving discussions. Lastly, *Stop, Think, and Discuss* poses a parting question for reflection. Parents or classroom staff can discuss these questions together, enabling them to be more clear and consistent as they respond to children's needs and behaviors.

The inspiration for the use of illustrations created here came from the work of Adele Faber and Elaine Mazlish in their book *How To Talk So Kids Will Listen and Listen So Kids Will Talk* (2001). The extensive use of illustrations in this book makes it possible to consider in visual and concrete terms two distinct approaches to responding to children's challenging behaviors and to reflect on the outcomes of each. This graphic element highlights how and why the problem-solving process, compared to more "typical" adult responses, is more effective in resolving children's conflicts. The illustrations and text intentionally simplify complicated events in order to make the interactions and strategies presented more accessible to readers. In this way, readers can more easily pinpoint the range of actions and emotions — of both adults and children — that make challenging conflicts so difficult to negotiate. My hope is that this clarity will give parents and teachers very accessible and concrete examples to explore and discuss.

The problem-solving version of the stories illustrated in this book here are based on actual experiences related by parents and teachers (some are condensed in order to fit into six panels). The stories are national and international, taking place in the program that I started in Massachusetts, The Giving Tree School in Gill, as well as programs in Fitchburg and Amherst, Massachusetts, New York City, Utah, Bookham and Bristol, England, and Cape Elizabeth, Maine. The illustrated "typical" responses are a composite of common adult reactions to children's problems, with no actual parent or classroom teacher in mind. In other words, the problem-solving approach illustrates the real-life situation as it occurred and the adult's actual response to the children involved. The "typical" situation is a fictionalized version of what is likely to happen when adults respond with a more traditional approach to children's conflict. The reason I wanted to present both approaches is to make the point that anyone can do things differently with a different set of strategies. It is possible to change our interactions with children, no matter what our past has been.

It is my hope that the illustrations of these "typical" strategies give readers a recognizable look at some of their own reactions to children, particularly those responses they'd like to change. (I know I see aspects of myself as a younger teacher in some of these scenarios!) It is also my hope that the problem-solving illustrations provide a quicker yet deeper way to understand more positive and effective responses, while also reviewing and extending the practice of the six problem-solving strategies.

* * * * *

Children are complex and sometimes mystifying beings. Each child possesses an individual spirit and presence in the world. Each child has his or her own nature and way of learning and reacting to the people and events around them. It's what makes them so uniquely dynamic — each has his or her own story to tell. In whatever role we play with children, parent or classroom teacher, it is important to understand the predictable characteristics of how most children grow and develop, and also to have a set of tools — strategies — for nurturing uniquely individual growth and development. Finding that balance of support and guidance is the challenge.

To marvel in the wonder of children, and then to know how to support their individual strengths and gifts is not, for most adults, something that comes naturally. We all must work at it, noticing our own needs to "make a child behave," rather than accepting their actions as a young child's attempt to communicate what they need and want. Adults who respond to these actions by guiding children with limit setting and problem solving — and then reflecting on what has happened in a conscious way — will be more effective at providing the sustenance children need to become remarkable individuals.

As you explore the illustrated stories, discussions, and questions posed within these pages, you will see that children are very capable of problem-solving, often to the astonishment of adults. Children's sensitivity, emerging empathy, and creative solutions are the reasons I remain dedicated to both the efforts of the children and the adults who support them. They are my heroes and heroines in a world seeking social harmony and connection. If you are new to this problem-solving approach, I encourage you to be persistent — you are learning together with your children. And to those of you who are extending your knowledge of problem solving, take a moment to congratulate yourself for being persistent and open to change. And to all of you, enjoy reflecting on your love of children, and marvel every day at their remarkable abilities. You too will have astonishing stories to tell. At all times, remember to keep your sense of humor as you explore and experience failures, successes, and growth, and discover the questions that remain. It is not important to be perfect every day at problem-solving with young children — it is only important to keep trying.

*Children are complex beings, each with his or her own story to tell. With a balance of adult support and guidance, they also become capable and creative problem solvers.*

# How to Read This Book

### Instructions for Reading Illustrated Scenarios

The scenarios found throughout this book may look much different than regular text, but you'll find that they actually read in a very similar way. As shown here, panels are meant to be read from left to right (see numbers 1 through 3), and each scenario extends over two pages.

Within each panel, the method is the same. Look at the blown-up example of panel three here: "word balloons" are also generally read from top to bottom, left to right (as shown with labels *a* through *c*). If a scenario or panel looks confusing, you should be able to follow these basic rules so that the dialogue maintains a natural flow.

Panel 3 (above)

## What If...?

*Two children are fighting over a shopping cart, pulling and hitting, and I didn't see what happened or who was playing with it first. What should I do? It seems that every day I have to help my children with this kind of squabble, and it's very frustrating. What's the matter with my children? Why don't they get along? How can I help them learn to do something other than grabbing and hitting when they want something?*

# 1. The Problem-Solving Steps

### A Typical Situation and Response...

### What Happened Here?

Adults should not be surprised that children are sometimes physical when responding to conflict. Since they are still learning how to express themselves verbally, children will grab, yell, and/or hit as they try to communicate how they are feeling and what they want. The good news is that there is nothing "the matter" with your children! It is normal and healthy for them to express their feelings.

And more good news: the skills children need for effective problem-solving (also called *negotiating*) — often thought to be too difficult for young children to master — can actually be easily learned when adults stay calm and involve children in talking through and solving conflicts.

### If you find yourself in a situation like this, consider these strategies:

| INSTEAD OF... | TRY THIS... |
|---|---|
| Instead of putting away toys children are fighting over, | ► Get on the children's level, put your hands on the toy, name feelings, and set limits on any hurtful behavior. Then ask calmly in a neutral voice, *What's the problem?* |
| Instead of telling children how to share, | ► Listen carefully to their description of the problem and repeat what they say. Then ask *the children* involved to think of solutions. |

**What is the reason...**
**...for adults to be patient and respond with a problem-solving approach each time there's a conflict?**

Children's understanding of how to communicate verbally is constructed over time, one experience at a time. Each child's "learning curve" is affected by a combination of factors: personality, family experiences, language skills, and feelings about their environment and the people in it. Some children quickly develop the ability to respond to conflicts in a collaborative and nonphysical way, finding relief in the nonjudgmental and safe approach. Others take a longer time to trust the problem-solving process — to fully understand how it empowers them to fulfill their needs. Fortunately, as the saying goes, *Childhood is not a race, it is a journey.* If adults regularly and consistently take an unhurried approach — using a calm voice, relaxing their bodies, and allowing time for children to express themselves and offer ideas — children will begin to respond to the predictable use of this approach.

As this happens, conflicts will become less emotionally charged. Once it is clear what the real problem is about (i.e., that both children want the toy, not that they are acting mean or naughty), then it is possible to take concrete steps to solve it. Young children think in concrete terms, so when they become accustomed to being asked for solutions, they are able and eager to offer them.

**A problem-solving response to the same situation:**

## The Problem-Solving Steps

1. Approach calmly, stopping any hurtful actions.
2. Acknowledge children's feelings.
3. Gather information.
4. Restate the problem.
5. Ask for ideas for solutions and choose one together.
6. Be prepared to give follow-up support.

### What Happened Differently This Time?

In this situation, the children were supported by an adult using the six problem-solving steps. First, the adult remained calm, setting limits as she approached (*...pulling needs to stop*) to prevent hurtful or destructive behavior, then got on the child's level (Step 1). This approach communicated a nonthreatening response, rather than adding the adult's emotions to an escalating situation. The adult then named feelings, accepting them without judgment, and "neutralized" the disputed object by holding it. This allowed children to focus their attention on the problem-solving process (Step 2). Once the children were calmer, the adult asked each child to describe the problem and listened carefully to their answers (Step 3). She restated what they said (Step 4) — further acknowledgment that their voices had been heard. Next, she asked them, *What can we do to solve this problem?* (Step 5). The children were thus reassured not only that their needs would be met, but that they would play a role in how this was accomplished.

With practice and experience, children become more expert at responding *verbally* to conflict and thinking of solutions that work for everyone. The children here quickly agreed on a solution, and the adult repeated it. She then supported their effort by saying *You solved the problem! You're sharing!* (Step 6). This type of encouragement helps children become aware of the effectiveness of their words.

### Something More to Consider...

Notice that in the second illustration, based on an actual situation, the adult placed her hands on the toy as she named children's feelings. This is a very valuable strategy — in fact, an essential strategy. Consider this: the child who is holding the toy does not have a problem…he has the toy! Since the child who has the toy may be focused on playing with it, he may not even notice that there is a problem. The child who has the toy has control of it, which is upsetting to the other child. Both children will have difficulty paying attention to the problem-solving process until control of the toy is in safe and neutral hands.

The simplest definition of *mediation* or *conflict resolution* is "the act of balancing power." The adult in this situation placed her hands on the toy and stated, *I'm going to hold this until we figure out the problem.* She did this calmly and slowly, watching to see the reaction of the child holding the toy. If a child does, in fact, become upset at the idea of relinquishing the toy to the adult, the adult can offer that they hold it together, and that the other child involved hold it with them. Once the object is either in the adult's "neutral" hands or in the hands of everyone together, the "power" is balanced and it is possible to focus on solutions.

### Stop, Think, & Discuss

*As you engage children in the use of problem-solving strategies, consider writing an anecdote or journal entry about what happens during each negotiation. Take note of changes in children's reactions as you name feelings and support children as they come up with solutions. Objective notes will show the individual growth that can occur when adults consistently respond to conflicts with problem solving. Adults will notice the growth in their own skills as well!*

*Two of my children want to use the same swing. One child gets there first and then the other child begins to shriek and cry because she can't use it. I find this very upsetting. I also don't like when children refuse to listen, talk back to me, or walk away while I'm talking. It's disrespectful. Why don't my children do a better job of sharing? I keep telling them that I want them to share and be friends, but it doesn't seem to be sinking in.*

## 2. I Want a Turn!

### A Typical Situation and Response...

### What Happened Here?

Young children "show" feelings by being loudly verbal and/or intensely physical. When children's feelings are ignored, those feelings often get louder and last longer. In this situation, Grace tried to reach the swing before Tamika but was too far away to get there first. When the adult did not respond to Grace's feelings, she became even more frustrated. Grace *really* wanted to use the swing, not another piece of playground equipment. In addition, the adult made an impossible request — telling Grace to *Be friends* with the child who had what she wanted. Unsupported by the adult, the child yelled *Leave me alone* and walked away. (More on "back talk," p. 62)

### If you find yourself in a situation like this, consider these strategies:

| INSTEAD OF... | TRY THIS... |
|---|---|
| Instead of trying to give upset children something else to do, | ► Set limits on potentially hurtful behaviors (*Pulling needs to stop*). |
| Instead of telling children to *Calm down, Be friends,* or *Use your words,* | ► Name feelings until children are calmer, and listen carefully to what they are saying, encouraging them to solve the problem. |

**What is the reason...**
**...to avoid saying things like *Calm down, Use your words,* or *Be friends*?**

Adults spend a lot of time helping children learn academic skills like reading, math, and answers to questions like *Why is the sky blue?* (I'm still working on the answer to that one). But often we just expect that children will *know* how to make friends. We forget that building successful relationships requires developing a complex set of skills, such as cause-and-effect thinking and being able to see things from another person's perspective. When strong emotions are involved, this process is even more challenging. Like any other kind of learning, acquiring social skills also requires practice. As one child approaches another, she has to figure out how to engage *that* child — should she smile, offer a toy, use specific words? When there is a conflict, what works then? A push, a shriek, a plea for help?

In deciding how to give support, adults need to consider that the words *calm down* tell a child to change their feelings. Remember, we can choose how we act, but not how we feel. In order to "be friends," children must have a *desire* to be friends. We can choose to act respectfully toward others, but we can't be made to like them. Sometimes adults also tell children *use your words,* but which ones? (Preschoolers know about 3000 words.) If parents and teachers use *problem-solving* words, children will learn to use *those* words.

**A problem-solving response to the same situation:**

### What Happened Differently This Time?

As the adult approached the child pulling on the swing, she quickly and calmly got down on the child's level, physically holding the child back and setting limits by saying *pulling must stop* (a more emphatic version of *pulling needs to stop*). Stopping hurtful behavior is an important first step. It is necessary that everyone feel safe before talking about solutions. The upset child understood from the adult's calm approach that she was trying to help. The adult then acknowledged the child's feelings, by saying *You're very frustrated;* this statement reinforced that the adult understood and let the child know the name of those feelings. The adult's acceptance of her feelings had a calming effect on the child, and the pulling stopped.

With adult support, it became possible for the two children to talk about the problem and offer solutions. Sometimes children quickly come up with ideas of how to resolve a problem, as the children did here. At other times, it may take more discussion and more exchange of ideas until they both agree on a solution. This conflict provided a dynamic opportunity for logical thinking about possible compromises. The solution even included important math skills like counting! The biggest difference in the adult's approach here, compared to a more usual response, was that she saw the conflict as an opportunity to support children's social and emotional growth.

## Something More to Consider...

Why does the child who has not initiated the conflict need to stop and interact with the other child? This is a frequently asked question. If one child clearly has the swing, why should that child be required to stop his or her activity to talk to a child who is screaming and grabbing to get it? It is important to recognize that this situation is a learning opportunity for both children. Our actions can upset others, even when that is not our intent. Understanding how we affect the feelings of others is an essential social skill that we can foster in preschool. By participating in the problem-solving process, the child on the swing is also learning that she can think of solutions to problems that can work for everyone.

Though it may seem on the surface that this approach risks reinforcing the hurtful behavior, it's important to remember that if we want children to learn new behaviors or strategies for getting their needs met, we need to recognize the opportunities that conflicts provide for teaching them these new social skills. When children don't speak up, adults often describe them as *unassertive* or *passive*. If adults don't want children to be passive, then we can be most effective by helping children actively learn to negotiate in a positive way as they solve life's everyday problems.

## Stop, Think, & Discuss

*How do you show emotions? When you are upset, do you say so directly, or do you express it by withdrawing or being grouchy or demanding? Most adults did not experience attention to their feelings as children, and they are consequently unsure about how to react to the feelings of others. When a child cries, is your reaction,* Come on — snap out of it!? *If so, discuss the reason for this response.*

## What If...?

*A child picks up a toy or a chair and throws it, or a child scratches a friend when he doesn't get what he wants. Shouldn't these actions lead to a time-out for that child? Aren't there certain behaviors that require strong action from the adult so that the child learns these behaviors are unacceptable and must stop?*

# 3. I Hate This Car!

### A Typical Situation and Response...

### What Happened Here?

When the child threw a car, the adult's initial (and appropriate) response was to stop the behavior. This was followed by a time-out, removing the child from the scene where she could not hurt others. However, this approach solved only part of the problem. It still wasn't clear why the child was upset to the point of throwing a car. Young children will be physical when upset — they don't yet know how to *say* what they feel or *describe* what they need. Adults make things worse by punishing *the child* instead of responding to his or her feelings and needs. Unrecognized angry feelings and unmet needs may lead to another, more dangerous action — in this case, throwing the chair during time-out.

### If you find yourself in a situation like this, consider these strategies:

| INSTEAD OF... | TRY THIS... |
|---|---|
| Instead of assuming that the child is being "bad" and punishing her, | ► Quickly and calmly get on the child's level and set limits on the action (throwing) that is unsafe. |
| Instead of ignoring the child's upset feelings, | ► Name those feelings, using a nonjudgmental tone. |

**What is the reason...**
**...that time-out and other punishment strategies have been discredited by early childhood specialists?**

Children are active explorers and active communicators; they learn best — and express most of their feelings — by *doing*. When young children are annoyed by a toy, they will probably show their annoyance through an obvious action and/or by making a loud noise. Adults need to stop children when they do unsafe things while also remembering that it is generally not the child's *intention* to be unsafe.

The latest guidelines for developmentally appropriate practice published by the National Association for the Education of Young Children (Copple & Bredekamp, 2009) emphasize reasoning together with children rather than reacting to their violations of rules with harsh discipline. Problem solving works because preschoolers are increasingly capable of expressing their needs and wants — and eventually their feelings — in words, as they develop an understanding of the consequences of their actions. In contrast, ineffective strategies include "punishing unacceptable behavior, refereeing disagreements, and repeatedly putting the same children in time-out or disciplining them in other ways unrelated to their actions" (p. 159). A time-out for inappropriate behavior may have little effect because it is not related to the underlying problem, fails to acknowledge and help children express their feelings, and does not help the child learn to problem-solve in a safe and collaborative way.

**A problem-solving response to the same situation:**

## What Happened Differently This Time?

In this problem-solving approach, the adult quickly stopped the child's unsafe behavior. By getting on the child's level, the adult was less threatening. Since the child didn't feel frightened or shamed by the adult, she was more able to listen when that adult set limits by saying *Throwing toys needs to stop. That might hurt someone.* This helped to make clear that the adult disliked the action of *throwing toys,* not the child or her feelings. The adult also gave reasons for the limit. A logical rather than punitive consequence then became possible: a problem-solving negotiation is a logical consequence. After initially setting limits, the adult began the problem solving by insisting on an agreement that throwing would stop. The problem solving that followed provided an active learning opportunity for both children. The adult understood the frustrated child's point of view, knowing that she did not intend to be "bad." With adult support and lots of practice, her impulse to "act out" frustration will eventually be replaced by the ability to *say* she is frustrated and that she has a problem.

Adults can be most helpful to children if they are calm themselves. In order to stay calm, parents and teachers can remind themselves that their children are not "bad," they just need new skills.

### Something More to Consider...

As we react to young children's behaviors, it important to consider how children learn best and what motivates them to stick with something until they have learned it. Can children actually *learn* in a time-out chair? If you wanted to learn a new language, how long would you need to sit alone in a chair (sorry, no language tapes allowed…)? Clearly, learning requires much more support than time-out chairs have to offer.

So let's think about how we *all* learn. Consider one of your own skills (e.g., cooking, singing, etc.). How did you become skilled? What motivated you to stay with an activity until you did it well? It is very likely that you acquired *confidence in your skills* because you were *enjoying* yourself while making *choices,* doing something of *personal interest,* and experiencing *success.* These are the five factors of *intrinsic* motivation, and they help all learners to develop long-term skills.

As we consider motivation factors, it is important to notice that fear and shame are not included. Children do not learn well when they are afraid of adults or sense that adults think poorly of them. Strong self-esteem is one of the most important ingredients needed to succeed as a learner. All children will make mistakes as they grow and learn (as adults do as well). If we are patient and give them time to practice new skills, they will indeed become successful problem solvers.

### Stop, Think, & Discuss...

*Think of something you tried to learn recently, such as a second language or a new hobby. How much time did it take you to become more confident? List the things that helped you to learn a new skill. Did you need someone to punish you for your errors? Or did factors such as developing confidence, enjoyment, success, and support make it easier to learn?*

## What If...?

*A child pushes another child, who then pushes back, and this has happened numerous times between these two children. It seems that there are certain pairs of children who get into a pattern of hurting each other. Sometimes they are siblings; sometimes they are friends. What do I do when I've problem-solved with them but their behavior doesn't change? Sometimes I think problem-solving with them just isn't working! What am I doing wrong?*

# 4. He Pushed Me!

### A Typical Situation and Response...

### What Happened Here?

Two children pushed each other again after problem-solving only moments before. The adult judged quickly that the earlier problem-solving effort had failed. However, it is interesting to note that the adult also quickly gave up on the problem-solving effort — shaming the children for not getting along — after just one try at solving the problem together! The adult's assumptions (*What's the matter with you?*) and body language (scolding and angry) were typical of a more authoritarian approach to conflict solutions. Neither the adult nor the children have learned yet how to craft a solution that is detailed enough to work, or how to keep problem-solving until the process works.

### If you find yourself in a situation like this, consider these strategies:

| INSTEAD OF... | TRY THIS... |
|---|---|
| Instead of giving up after trying to problem-solve once or twice, | ► Approach the children with calm body language and set limits again. Understand that problem solving is an ongoing learning process that will improve with practice, like learning to write your name or play an instrument. |
| Instead of accepting vague solutions like *We'll share,* | ► Ask *What does that mean you will do? What will that look like?* |

## What is the reason...
## ...that children sometimes repeat a behavior right after being told to stop?

Very few people — whether children or adults — do something well after just one try. Parents and teachers need to practice their role as children's learning partners, being patient with them as well as with themselves for as long as it takes. Similarly, some children require many opportunities before they learn problem-solving words and trust that the adult will try to respond to conflicts this way *every time.* Other children are more interested in finding solutions, and after just a few tries, become quite expert at coming up with solutions for everyone (as seen in the problem-solving scenario, p. 21).

When adults support children to problem-solve, there are two sets of learners — the children and the adults. After each problem-solving situation, adults need to think about what worked and what didn't. Did you get down on children's level? Did you fully listen to and name feelings? Did you ask the *children* for solutions? Give yourself *a month or two* of practicing how to problem-solve before expecting to feel confident in this process. Try to maintain a calm attitude; assume that if you don't understand a particular problem between children, you will if you keep trying. In addition, when adults patiently support conflict negotiations, children learn about diverse points of view and varied solutions.

**A problem-solving response to the same situation:**

### What Happened Differently This Time?

As the adult approached here, she stayed calm despite the recurrence of conflict between the two children. She got down on the children's level, stopped the hurting, stated limits, and simply problem-solved again. Because the adult was patient and nonthreatening, the children did not feel frightened or distracted, and they shared more honestly with her (*I did [push] cuz he's not letting me be here like we said*). It is very important to notice that one child, after showing his feelings by pushing, did actually *say* his feelings (*I'm angry too…*). This is often the developmental progression: children use the old behavior and, once support has arrived, they use the new one. If adults support learning that happens in small increments, the new behavior becomes more consistent, as the former patterns fade away.

The adult here also kept the children in charge of solutions by asking for details. It is important to note that the first negotiated solution (not shown here) was not detailed enough. The adult's role is to ask clarifying questions about solutions. When children suggest vague solutions like *We'll share* or *We'll take turns,* adults can help them create a visual picture of the solution by asking questions such as *When you share, what will that look like?* or *How will you know which is his space?* With practice, children's solutions will become more detailed and effective.

## Something More to Consider...

What are you thinking as you approach a conflict? What is your body language? This is exactly where adult learning and change must begin. As you learn to problem-solve, it will also help you to examine your response and the very first thing you say as a problem erupts. Are you repeating phrases you heard as a child or have picked up from others, such as *What's the matter with you?!* or *How would you like it if someone did that to you?!* Shocked by children's behaviors, do you blurt out *You're making such a big fuss!* or *Cheer up…It's not that bad!*? When we examine our personal histories and consider *our* feelings about conflict, we come to understand our reactions more clearly. If, for example, our emotional needs as children were not met by the adults around us, we need to be very aware of how this past experience affects us now in our own interactions with children. Consider how your childhood discipline experiences might be affecting your approach to conflict. Make a clear decision not to simply do what was done to you but to act according to your goals for your children. Changing your approach doesn't mean the past was completely wrong, it only means that you want to be more effective and successful with the children in your life.

## Stop, Think, & Discuss

*When I was a young child I went out in the rain and played in a puddle (fun!). My Mom took me inside, said I was* naughty, *and sat me on the stairs. I had no idea what I had done. I wondered,* She doesn't like mud…or me? *Discuss something you did as a child that upset adults and what you needed from the adults around you when they responded.*

## What If...?

*Children can sometimes become very upset when they are separating from a parent or family member. It's difficult to calm them down when they are so emotional. When I try to reassure or distract them, it works for a little while but often doesn't last. Even worse, I have a child who gets so upset after his mother leaves that he yells at me or kicks me. Even when children finally do stop crying in these situations, sometimes the smallest thing can set them off again. What can I do to make them stop crying?*

# 5. Noo! Don't Go!

### A Typical Situation and Response...

### What Happened Here?

A child separating from a parent or family member is very vulnerable and may become intensely emotional. There are no correct, "big boy" emotions that go with this moment. Dylan, already upset, became even more upset when taken from his mother by the teacher. Her "fix-it" approach (*It's okay — let's do a puzzle.*) probably made the situation worse, as Dylan's feelings were completely ignored. While the adult was trying to be helpful, this kind of comment communicated to the child that the adult did not realize how painful his feelings were: he was being left behind!

### If you find yourself in a situation like this, consider these strategies:

| INSTEAD OF... | TRY THIS... |
|---|---|
| Instead of ignoring feelings and trying to get the child to stop crying, | ► Name the child's feelings directly, understanding the intensity of separation feelings. Encourage the child to "empty out" those feelings. |
| Instead of scolding children for being emotional, | ► Consider how scary it is to feel abandoned and not know when — or if — a parent will return. |
| Instead of thinking your job is to stop the child's crying, | ► Think of this as an active learning moment. Help the child connect the feeling with a word that names it. |

## What is the reason...
## ...that it is so important to notice and name children's feelings?

Very young children will typically show their feelings by being physical. In the first situation, the child kicked the adult, as if to say, *Now, do you get how upset I am?* This reaction is not at all a result of conscious thinking on the part of the child — in fact, it doesn't involve thinking at all. Overwhelmed by emotion, children do not know how to *say* they are angry or sad. The adult's role is to help children become aware of their feelings and learn the words to name them. Eventually they will be able to *say* feelings instead of *physically show* them.

Parents and teachers may have reservations about saying something like *You're sad,* unsure that this is really the emotion a child is feeling. What if they're feeling *mad* instead? When unsure, adults may say, *You look upset...you're crying. Upset* is a general word that describes many emotions, and it can be a useful place to start. It is, however, very important over time to describe emotions specifically so that children can hear a variety of words that describe their feelings. For these words to sink in and be comforting enough to help calm a child who is upset, adults must repeat them calmly. At first the child hears only a soothing voice and then, as calming happens, hears and understands words that are reassuring.

**A problem-solving response to the same situation:**

## What Happened Differently This Time?

Both adults here stayed calm and saw the situation from the child's point of view. They avoided belittling the child's feelings (by not saying something like *Come on, be a big boy…it's okay*) and showed that they understood what it must be like for a child not to have control over what is happening — it's scary! When children sense that an adult understands how hard a particular moment can be, it is deeply comforting and builds trust. In this situation, the child first heard that the adult was paying very close attention to his feelings and valuing them. Both adults also immediately *described* the child's feelings in a calm voice, communicating that they respected and accepted those feelings. This is profoundly reassuring. Children may calm immediately, as this child did, or the adult may need to repeat several times the emotions they are sensing.

If parents and teachers remain consistent as they name feelings in different situations, children will come to trust that adults understand their anxiety. Keep in mind that in a situation like this, children are struggling to understand if they are safe. Feeling safe is the result of *experiencing safety a number of times,* not simply being told *You are safe.* Children don't know they will be safe away from the parent *and* that the parent will actually come back until this has happened numerous times.

## Something More to Consider...

Sometimes children can react very strongly to separation, becoming intensely upset. They may even become physically ill. This is not an "overreaction" to the situation — the child being left behind may actually feel terrified. It is important for parents and teachers to know that separation anxiety is real and not unusual in the early years. It requires a patient and warm response. Thoughtful planning by the parent and teacher — with consideration given to how and when the separation will happen — will help enormously. Parents can help by sharing the plan with their child in advance, offering a simple explanation. For example, parents might say, *We will walk in together. We will read one book. Then I will give you a big hug and say goodbye.* As the parent leaves, it is important that he or she hands the child over to the teacher with the reassurance that the parent will return and an indication of when that will happen. Teachers should *not* remove a child from the parent. This could cause the child to think that the teacher is taking the child *against the parent's wishes,* which indeed would be very frightening. Once the parent is gone, the teacher should be prepared to focus on the child, naming the child's feelings until he or she has calmed, and offering physical comfort if the child wants it.

## Stop, Think, & Discuss

*How can parent-child separations be handled compassionately? Discuss a plan specific to your child's and the program's needs in advance, including a plan for the very moment of separation. Teachers must avoid "peeling" the child from the parent, and parents must not ask teachers to do this. Discuss the importance of naming a child's feelings, and think about whether you are doing it often enough.*

## What If...?

*A child becomes very frustrated while working with materials and appears to need help. Should I wait to see what happens or should I approach the child to find out what the problem is and offer help? Sometimes if I do go over to offer help, the child begins acting out by kicking or throwing the materials and shouting at me. When I try to set limits or make suggestions, things seem to get worse.*

# 6. Go Away!

### A Typical Situation and Response...

### What Happened Here?

In this situation, Jamal was frustrated with block building as the adult approached and asked, *What's wrong?* She then insisted that Jamal look at her while she was speaking. There are two points of view here: the adult's and the child's. Jamal was already experiencing a challenging moment when the adult made two demands of him — to answer her question and to *look* at her. Motivated by what she wanted to know and how she expected Jamal to respond, the adult neglected to focus on Jamal's needs and feelings. Jamal, already frustrated with the blocks, was unable to respond to these new demands and the situation got worse.

### If you find yourself in a situation like this, consider these strategies:

| INSTEAD OF... | TRY THIS... |
|---|---|
| Instead of assuming that children must make eye contact in order to listen to you, | ► Accept the variety of ways that children use eye contact and know that it is very likely, even without eye contact, that they are listening. |
| Instead of asking *What's wrong?* | ► Take this opportunity to join the child in problem solving. Place yourself nearby and on the child's level in order to talk and listen easily. |

**What is the reason...**
**...to avoid telling children, *Look at me when I'm talking to you*?**

Adults sometimes think that getting children to look at them will help children focus on the problem, but this expectation often makes the situation worse. The demand that young children shift their attention away from what they perceive as the problem is not a developmentally appropriate request because most young children do not make lengthy eye contact with *anyone*. Instead, young children use their eyes to scan their surroundings for interesting objects and actions. Watch children when they are trying to listen — often they will either fix their gaze on something distant or their gaze will drift about randomly. Since it is hard for young children to keep more than one thing in mind at a time, relaxing their eyes in this way may help children use their ears to *listen* more effectively. Children begin making more eye contact as they grow older and become more interested in conversations, rather than materials and actions.

Secondly, some children grow up in families and/or cultures where eye contact is avoided, or perhaps even discouraged, between the younger and older members of a family. If making eye contact is contrary to a child's family experience, adults may create cultural misunderstandings and even embarrassment if eye contact is demanded of a child. Positioning yourself next to instead of in front of a child may seem less confrontational to some children.

**A problem-solving response to the same situation:**

### What Happened Differently This Time?

When Jamal's building fell, the adult observed and responded from Jamal's perspective, approaching him calmly, getting on his level, and quietly reaching out to him with no demands. Right away, before any words were spoken, Jamal sensed from the adult's body language that she was going to support him. By simply naming the feelings she perceived, the adult showed Jamal that she accepted his emotions, whatever they were. At this point Jamal felt that his feelings were recognized and understood, and he began to calm and to talk about the situation. From here, it was easier for the adult to assist him as he tried to build with the blocks again. Since the adult named and really listened to his feelings, Jamal also learned about a feeling called *frustrated,* and his trust in adults likely increased. He also learned that there is nothing "wrong" with blocks falling. It's merely a problem to be solved — and that problems can be a chance to work together!

## Something More to Consider...

Most children are very sensitive to physical details. As a result they notice adult body language before they even hear what the adult is saying. As adults approach challenging situations, it is very useful to consciously maintain a calm expression and relaxed body so that children do not immediately become defensive, resulting in an escalation of the problem. Even when adults remain calm, children who have previously experienced an authoritarian approach may continue to be defensive until they trust you and your calm manner. Over time, a nonthreatening approach — a relaxed face, a gentle tone of voice, and most importantly, willingness to be on children's level — will help children to calm more quickly. As you approach, notice if your hands are on your hips even when you are actually trying *not* to be authoritarian! Old habits are hard to change. When we use body language that communicates the same message as our words, children are reassured. Placing yourself at the child's level is a clear and quick way to show that you are ready to offer help rather than make demands. As you get on the child's level, offer a reassuring hand to a shoulder, and notice how it is received — some children don't want physical contact. Your calm, predictable presence can be enough.

## Stop, Think, & Discuss

*Consider when and how you make eye contact with others. Watch your children and notice how they use eye contact as a way of understanding the world. Notice differences between individuals, whether they are children or adults. Some cultures have a tradition of not making eye contact. Respecting differences is essential to a nonbiased approach to communication.*

# What If...?

*A younger and an older child have a conflict about sharing. Whose side should I take? Older children are so much more able to say what they want, and they sometimes try to dominate the younger children. On the other hand, shouldn't the younger children be made to share? How else will they learn that they can't always have what they want just because they are crying? No matter whose side I take, it doesn't seem to turn out well.*

# 7. No! Miiine!

### A Typical Situation and Response...

### What Happened Here?

The adult in this situation became "Decider" instead of "Mediator." Her response to the situation was to try to fix it by first telling the younger child that she needed to share and then preventing the older child from taking his turn when he became demanding. By taking one child's side and then the other's, the adult did not support either child or make the situation better. Though the adult probably wanted to "keep everyone happy," she created more confusion *and* missed a teachable moment. The younger child still does not know how to respond to turn-taking requests, and the older child became even more frustrated with the younger one when she refused to share.

### If you find yourself in a situation like this, consider these strategies:

| INSTEAD OF... | TRY THIS... |
|---|---|
| Instead of assuming that young children cannot express themselves, | ► Stay calm and watch their body language in order to understand the problem. |
| Instead of assuming that older children will dominate, | ► Describe that a problem is happening, and ask the children to come up with a solution. |

### What is the reason…
### …to stay neutral and not take sides?

It may sometimes seem to adults that children who can barely talk need someone on their side, and they do in fact need extra verbal help. Adults can respond to a young child's brief statements (e.g., *Miiine!* and *Me lap*) by expanding on the child's words (e.g., *D'Asaya, you want guinea in your lap and Zaquawn wants to pet him*). To be effective at supporting children as they learn to problem-solve, adults need to stay neutral, unbiased by children's age or language differences, and uncritical of the solution the children agree on. Adults who remain neutral give equal support to everyone involved by providing words only for children's wants or needs.

As mediators, adults also show their neutrality when they accept the feelings of children who have more advanced language abilities. Their needs should not be discounted just because they are older or because "they should know better." Conflict resolution between children of different ages and abilities, facilitated by neutral adults, will result in an active learning experience in communicating needs and wants, and a chance for children to practice finding solutions. The answer to the question of *When will children learn?* or *When should I start mediating?* is as soon as a child can indicate *yes* or *no* and communicate wants and needs with body language.

**A problem-solving response to the same situation:**

## What Happened Differently This Time?

In this actual problem-solving response, the adult listened to both children, describing the problem and the children's feelings. This let the children know that she was listening to both of them and not taking sides. By placing herself in a neutral position between them, the adult also "showed" her neutrality in a physical way. Keeping a very calm tone of voice, she repeated the problem so it was clear and then asked both children, *What can we do to solve this problem?* Don't assume that less verbal children are unable to think of solutions. Frequently, they will indicate a solution nonverbally, and they will surprise you! For example, if two children are fighting over a toy, one child might take another toy from the shelf and hand it (or the original toy) to the other child. This is a way of saying *I can play with this one and you can play with the other!* In this conflict involving the guinea pig, the older child did offer a very creative "win-win" solution. Actually it was a win-win-win solution, for the two children and the adult.

It is a natural response for a child who wants something to try to dominate another with size or height. And screaming and crying is to be expected from children who have as yet undeveloped language abilities. Repeated experiences that give children of *all* abilities a chance to practice negotiation, will help all children grow in their ability to communicate and solve problems.

## Something More to Consider...

Adults often think they need to *give* children solutions until they are "old enough" to come up with them on their own. When and how will that happen? We've considered how children learn and what motivates them to learn (p. 17). If we accept that they need to be "active" in this process of finding a solution, we need to consider our supporting role. If we want children to write their names, would we do it *for* them? If we did, children would know that those are *our letters,* and they might lose confidence in themselves. Children need to use whatever abilities *they* have and build from there. This means initially scribbling or making very approximate letters. With practice, these writing attempts become increasingly successful.

Similarly, we can give children a list of solutions, but they will not feel ownership of those solutions. When children practice the thinking that is part of problem-solving, they become increasingly successful at crafting effective solutions. If adults stay calm and engage children in actively figuring out a solution together, children gradually become more practiced at finding solutions on their own. Their first attempts may be shaky and adults may need to say, *That's one idea of what we can do. Let's keep thinking of other ideas.* Follow-up questions about how children will carry out their proposed solutions can also help them think of alternative ideas and options.

## Stop, Think, & Discuss

*In order to be a "neutral" adult — ready to listen to all children (even those who have been hurtful) — it is important to be aware of one's own emotions. Think about what children say or do that make you particularly upset. Discuss how to make an "I" statement in those situations in order to calm yourself (see p. 69). Adults will mediate most successfully when they are calm and able to be neutral.*

## What If...?

*Two children are playing together, and they exclude another child who wants to join them. They shouldn't be allowed to do this, right? It's so upsetting to see or hear children rejecting another child. Sometimes they can be so mean to one other. How will children learn to include everyone in their play if I don't insist on it? How can I help them to be nicer to one another?*

# 8. We Don't Like Him!

### A Typical Situation and Response...

### What Happened Here?

The two boys threatening *You can't come to my football game!* are basically saying *Help! We're frustrated and we don't know how to handle this!* Young children have difficulty *asking* directly for what they want and *saying* their feelings in a gracious way. Instead the boys used a concrete threat to communicate their feelings: *You can't come to our football game!* The adult took this literally (*I know you all play football together*) and missed the point — the point is the *feeling*, not the football game. When Aiden was forced to give up his hammer, his frustration became anger, directed now at the adult.

### If you find yourself in a situation like this, consider these strategies:

| INSTEAD OF... | TRY THIS... |
|---|---|
| Instead of taking children's threats literally, | ► Figure out and name the feeling contained inside the threat. |
| Instead of forcing children to play together, | ► Encourage them to resolve the conflicts so all of their needs are met. |
| Instead of expecting that young children include others in their play, | ► Give support until you are sure they can play cooperatively. |

### What is the reason...
### ...children say things like *You can't come to my football game* (or *birthday party*) or *You're not my friend anymore*?

Children are usually not subtle communicators — when they are upset, they use words that are likely to have "punch" (be glad that the punch is verbal, not physical!) Children use concrete threats when they are trying to express feelings. Think of the threat as the "wrapping" around the feeling. *You can't come to my football game* usually means *I am mad!* It is important for adults not to take the statement literally but rather to listen closely to the *intended meaning:* anger. If we can respond to the emotion rather than the threat, the threat will most likely not be repeated.

Sometimes children say *You're not our friend...You can't play here,* which usually means *We want to play alone.* It can be very effective to state for them the underlying message: *It sounds to me like you're upset and you want to play alone, is that right?* Sometimes it is possible to negotiate another option: *Would you tell us what you're doing? Maybe we can figure out how to do it together?* But sometimes we need to listen to children and support their terms of play. The choices they've made for play, at least for right now, may be all they can manage successfully given the level of their social skills and developmental abilities.

**A problem-solving response to the same situation:**

## What Happened Differently This Time?

In this problem-solving situation, the adult did not take the children's threats of exclusion literally. The two boys with the hammers initially did not want to interrupt the fun they were having together — or have to give up a hammer — by including another child. Sometimes, children can really only manage to play successfully with one other child. Or sometimes the materials are limited, and children don't immediately see how they can all work together. The adult understood that the *football game* statement was meant to shout out strong feelings. Without repeating the threat, the adult named the "inside" message of that statement, *You sound really angry,* and the threats stopped. Once the three boys decided on what each of them would do (i.e., hammer or hand out nails) they resumed play with *their* version of being friends (playing together). The adult provided neutral problem-solving support, and the children decided how to work it out.

### Something More to Consider...

Children, like adults, make mistakes. They spill milk and break things. They say hurtful things, like *You're not my friend anymore,* which are a "mistaken" way of saying *I'm upset with you!!* We can think of these "mistakes" — whether accidental or intentional — as explorations or "oops" moments.

Children make mistakes for different reasons. Some mistakes happen simply due to a lack of experience. Daniel Gartrell (1994) calls these *experimentation* mistakes (p. 37). Children also imitate the mistaken behaviors of others, such as exclusion, swear words, or name-calling. Gartrell calls these *socially-influenced* mistakes (p. 37). Children can also engage in more extreme behaviors, by being repeatedly aggressive towards others or by regularly expressing a desire to hurt themselves. Gartrell calls these episodes *strong needs* mistaken behavior — the result of strong underlying unmet needs (p. 38). This type of mistake is different from experimentation and socially-influenced mistakes because of its *intensity* and *frequency* (p. 43). A child who throws a chair once may be having a hard day. A child who is consistently dangerous to others in some way or routinely says *I hate myself* is a child who has very strong needs. When adults keep this framework in mind, it becomes easier to have the patience, energy, and understanding to give children the support they need.

### Stop, Think, & Discuss

*Discuss how you can support children's developing sense of fairness. Is "fairness" a rule you can impose on children or is it a concept they need to explore on their own through trial and error? If adults always ask children to choose from a list of "fair" solutions, how will children learn to create solutions independently or fairly? If you had to use someone else's solution, would this seem "fair"?*

## What If...?

*A bossy child always tries to take toys from other, quieter children, insisting that he had it first. He gets very tense, demanding things in a loud, threatening voice, always wanting his way immediately. Even if he did have something first, I don't want to reward the behavior by giving in. But when I try to stop the behavior, things only seem to get worse! How do I teach my children that they can't just go up to others and grab things? And how do I help those children who are not very assertive and just give in?*

# 9. I Got It First!

### A Typical Situation and Response...

### What Happened Here?

The immediate reaction of this adult was to judge which child "had it first" and which one was a "bully." It was very hard for the adult to support Anouk — though he was very much in need of support. Instead, she sided with Dyani, telling Anouk that he was *not nice.* The adult also did not respond to Anouk's frustrated feelings, which became so intense he began kicking another truck. Seeing this, Dyani became scared and offered to give up the truck he was using. He may have worried that Anouk would be after him next. Better to give up the truck before that happened!

### If you find yourself in a situation like this, consider these strategies:

| INSTEAD OF... | TRY THIS... |
|---|---|
| Instead of assuming the loudest child is a "bully," | ► Say *I can see there's a problem...* |
| Instead of taking sides when you hear *I had it first,* | ► Say to children, *You're saying you had it first and you're saying you had it first...* no matter what you think actually happened. |
| Instead of trying to control or stop intense feelings, | ► Name feelings repeatedly until the child calms. |

**What is the reason...**
**...to problem-solve even when you are certain that one child had a toy first?**

In order for children to play successfully, they need to know how to handle conflict — and here's a chance to practice problem-solving! This is far more important than who had something "first."

Adults often want to cultivate in children the social skills they *don't* see, like the ability to be assertive (if they have a quiet child like Dyani) or to be patient (if they have a more impatient child like Anouk). Interestingly, in this situation Dyani was being patient and Anouk was being assertive! If the adult stays neutral and helps them to talk, Dyani and Anouk will model these traits for each other.

Adults are most effective in supporting children's social skills when they show confidence in children's ability to learn from the conflict dialogue. If Dyani is going to become more assertive, it is important that we don't take over his chance to try it out. He cannot be forced to be assertive, but the adult can create a safe opening for him to say what he wants — and hope that he will step into that space and speak up for himself. Anouk also needs a chance to find out that negotiating is more effective than simply grabbing what he wants. By problem-solving and being patient, he eventually got the truck he wanted *and* he learned a specific strategy he can use next time (see p. 41).

**A problem-solving response to the same situation:**

## What Happened Differently This Time?

The adult in this alternative situation immediately used the word *problem*. This word signaled to the children that the adult would not take sides and would listen to both of them, which she did. She also named Anouk's feelings right away *and more than once*. Anouk's loud voice and demanding words showed the intensity of his frustration. The best way to help Anouk to become calmer (and develop patience) was for the adult to *be* calm and patient, letting him know that he was being heard. When Anouk heard his feelings named by the adult, he fully emptied out those feelings (*I got this first and I get it!*) and was then better able to explain his problem. The adult helped to clarify the real source of Anouk's frustration — the broken wheels on the fire truck — by repeatedly describing his feelings and then restating the problem: *So, Anouk, you want a truck that works and Dyani is still using it.* This was an essential clarification of the problem.

The adult also did not take sides over the issue of who had it "first." She simply accepted both children's claims. It is important to acknowledge these claims, without deciding who is "right," even if you think you are certain who had it first (I know...this is hard to do!). Remember that determining who had something "first" is not as important at the moment as helping children to practice new social skills.

## Something More to Consider...

There are a few issues to consider when children claim *But I had it first!*

Adults often ask, *Why should a child have to talk about a problem if that child had the toy first? Isn't that punishing a child who did nothing wrong?* In addition, they wonder if forcing the child who has the toy to problem-solve may reinforce the other child's demanding behavior. This does seem logical on the surface: *Children shouldn't get their way if they haven't asked nicely,* right? We *all* want to "get our way" or have our needs met. How are children going to learn to ask nicely for what they need if we don't take this opportunity to facilitate a new way of communicating?

Sometimes at the beginning of a conflict, adults think an easy way to solve it is to ask, *Who had it first?* Beware! Children have a variety of meanings for *first,* for example, *I was just using it* (or *I was using it yesterday*), *so I had it* first, or *I had it* first *cuz I like it and I* want *it!* Avoid this sticky reasoning, and accept all perspectives. Refusing to decide who had it first will keep you from being the "bad guy" who favors one child over another. Staying neutral is the easiest (and most effective) way to go.

## Stop, Think, & Discuss

*Are there children you particularly like or dislike? We all have preferences. List personality traits that you like and dislike in children. Think about how your attitudes may be affecting your behavior towards certain children. When children experience constant disapproval, their self-esteem suffers. Keeping in mind that personality is not a choice, discuss changes you can make to create a positive environment for all your children.*

## What If...?

*One of my children "freaks out" at the thought of me leaving the room as she waits for her Dad to arrive. If I have something important to do, like changing the baby, she becomes very unreasonable and just doesn't want to leave my side. What kinds of things can I do so children don't get so upset whenever I have to move away from them, even for a few minutes?*

# 10. Wait With Me!

### A Typical Situation and Response...

### What Happened Here?

Maribel was very excited about Dad arriving at the end of the day. At the same time, Lena was badly in need of having her diaper changed. The adult here focused on Lena's obvious physical needs and did not take the time to understand Maribel's need for the adult to wait with her. As a result, the adult labeled the child as *ridiculous* and ignored her feelings. The situation worsened as Maribel became angry at the adult as well as the baby.

### If you find yourself in a situation like this, consider these strategies:

| INSTEAD OF... | TRY THIS... |
|---|---|
| Instead of assuming the child's emotional demands are unimportant, | ► Identify and name the emotional aspect of what the child is saying. |
| Instead of labeling a child's demands as *ridiculous,* | ► Describe what the child is asking for and state again what you need to do. |
| Instead of ignoring the escalating problem, | ► Ask the child to think of a solution that will work for both of you. |

**What is the reason...**
**...to negotiate with a child who is being "unreasonable"?**

Though we sometimes think children are being "unreasonable," there are always reasons for children's behavior. Sometimes it is hard to figure out why a child gets suddenly upset over a situation that seems ordinary and routine. Maribel was anxious for her father to come and pick her up, but for reasons that the adult did not yet understand, she didn't want to wait alone. Adults can only problem-solve in these situations by initially identifying and respecting a child's *feelings,* rather than looking for logical reasons.

In this true story, Maribel, who was later diagnosed as very near-sighted, felt quite frightened when people moved out of sight (which can also happen to children without vision impairment). Over time, she learned to negotiate for the closeness to adults that she needed, even though she could not explain *why* she needed it. It never occurred to her that her vision was any different than anyone else's.

There will, of course, be times that adults cannot meet a child's *every* need. We can, however, describe the problem, name feelings, and try to meet the child's *emotional* needs. When children's *feelings* are supported and they are given choices, they are more likely to make a "reasonable" choice.

## A problem-solving response to the same situation:

### What Happened Differently This Time?

The adult here, though busy with necessary tasks, was willing to try to see the situation from the child's point of view. Children are not small adults. They are often experiencing challenges that they cannot explain. The adult here paid attention to Maribel's *feelings* even though she couldn't fully understand the child's *reasons*. The adult described the situation from the child's point of view and her own point of view — both are equally important. As the adult described that Maribel did not want to be alone and that Lena must have her diaper changed, she asked the child to come up with ideas for solving the problem. Clearly, Maribel is feeling out of control and insecure. The offer of control — the opportunity to make a choice about how to solve the problem — helped with this need. It also gave Maribel a chance to practice creating solutions that worked for the adult, the baby, and herself — a "win-win-win" situation! The adult's support strategies were simple: she described Maribel's feelings and the baby's needs, and she asked Maribel for a solution for both. Maribel rose to the challenge! Maribel needed to solve this sort of dilemma for quite a while until the adults in her life understood her disability. The additional positive result was that Maribel became quite an expert at finding solutions!

### Something More to Consider...

Though some children may appear to behave "unreasonably," children generally act out of a particular need, which is reflected in their behavior. As adults, we must consider how to respond when we don't understand the nature of a child's underlying need or how serious it is. Adding to the difficulty is the fact that most children are unable to explain what their need is — instead they shout, cry, bite, withdraw, etc. A child may be frightened to stay alone (like Maribel) because she can't see well. A child may refuse to put on a coat or sit close to others because touch causes a sensory overload (e.g., children with sensory integration disorder or those who have suffered abuse). Some children may react intensely in loud situations because of a recent loud trauma or a hearing problem. Other children may be reluctant to join activities because they don't know how to "read" social cues (e.g., children with autism spectrum disorder or those who simply lack social experience).

There are many reasons and emotions embedded in children's behaviors. It will take time for adults to sensitively observe a child in a variety of situations before the underlying reason behind a particular behavior becomes apparent. The most effective strategy is for adults to be as respectful and flexible with children's feelings as possible, while also stating our limits and needs. Problem solving can be a powerful way to work through even seemingly "unreasonable" situations.

### Stop, Think, & Discuss

*Think about a child you have known whose challenging behaviors and needs took a long time for you to understand. How did your perceptions of that child change once you knew the reasons for his or her behavior? Discuss what it would be like to have a constant earache but not be able to explain it to anyone — or even know that it was a problem that warranted explanation!*

## What If...?

*I have children who only want to play with each other; they refuse to let other children join their play. When they exclude someone, that child gets upset and then the situation escalates. Over and over I hear children say to one another,* You're not my friend! *and I try to tell them that we are all friends, but it doesn't seem to help. Sometimes children will state with clear reasoning why they don't want to play with a particular child (e.g.,* She bosses us*), but how will they learn to play together if I let them exclude someone?*

# 11. You're Not My Friend Anymore!

### A Typical Situation and Response...

### What Happened Here?

Two children were playing together successfully, sharing ideas and materials — quite an accomplishment for two egocentric preschoolers! Another child wanted to join in, but one of the children did not like this idea. If children were to politely say, *Sorry, the maximum amount of socializing that we can manage right now is with two people. Please don't take it personally,* adults would be thrilled and probably shocked! Instead, they say in their own preschool way, *Go away...You're not my friend!* The adult here responded by telling the children to *Be friends,* then said *Use your words* to Tasha and walked away before any solution had been found.

### If you find yourself in a situation like this, consider these strategies:

| INSTEAD OF... | TRY THIS... |
|---|---|
| Instead of restating a rule such as *We are all friends* or making a general suggestion like *Use your words* (which ones?), | ► Recognize that children are saying they are upset, and make a simple statement: *It sounds like there's a problem.* |
| Instead of forcing children to play together or avoiding a problem situation entirely, | ► Gather information, use specific language, and accept children's perspectives. |

**What is the reason...**
**...to listen to children's reasoning when they are excluding someone? Shouldn't they learn to be friends?**

If children could learn the skills of friendship simply by being told a rule, such as *Be friends,* the whole world would be a much friendlier place. Most children have the *desire* to be friends, but many don't have the social skills — yet — to make it happen easily. Instead of citing rules or using vague directives like *Use your words* or *Work it out,* adults can support friendships by closely watching and listening to children. By asking for and restating specific information, adults can understand where children are in their social and emotional development and what kind of support they need to develop friendships.

Observation and listening help us to see children becoming skilled at friendship — one child and one successful play experience at a time. The phrase *making* friends says it all: friendship is *constructed* in the course of multiple and enjoyable experiences. Adding to the challenge, the process of making friends is different from person to person. During each play experience, the child discovers the give-and-take process: What happens when I say this, when I do this, and when I play with two friends instead of one? Our adult role is to scaffold that construction, supporting each stage of growth until the friendship stands on its own — and so that it still works when there are three friends instead of two.

**A problem-solving response to the same situation:**

## What Happened Differently This Time?

The adult in this situation did not arrive with a preset agenda of expecting the children to "be friends" or to know how to use their words without support. Instead, his goal was to give the children practice using specific problem-solving words and some of the negotiating skills that can lead to friendship. The adult here recognized an opportunity to hear from the children involved what they wanted and which elements of the play situation they considered negotiable (in this case, an extra doll and a space somewhere else).

As a result of the problem-solving, the children understood that name-calling was not okay, that *You're not my friend anymore!* means *I'm angry,* that *bossing* people is not a behavior other people like, and that they were capable of coming up with a solution that worked for everyone. In other words, the adult accepted each child's level of social development and abilities and worked with each one — success was *scaffolded* by the adult for each child. One child was able only to say *Play somewhere else,* while another was able to point out *There's a baby over there.* The third, excluded, child was able to put both suggestions together and find a solution. With emerging social confidence, the children might next time *choose* to include another child. Likewise, a child might learn to ask, instead of demand, to be included in the play of others.

## Something More to Consider...

Very few situations involving children upset adults as much as those in which children exclude other children. Adults quickly become impatient and directive, typically taking the side of the "excluded" child, forcing inclusion, or leaving the children to thrash it out. The reason for this is that almost all of us have experienced the devastating pain of being excluded. And because of this emotional reaction, we don't always respond in a rational way, often missing the opportunity to actually help children learn the "how-to" of including others.

In order to support the construction of friendship, be prepared for the common things that children say (e.g., *We want to play alone* or *We don't like her*) until they learn new ways to negotiate. This is where the adults come in — it's important to listen, set limits on name-calling or hurtful words, and reflect back *feelings*. For example, *You're not my friend anymore!* was reflected back by the adult with *You sound really angry.* Interestingly, after the adult named Tasha's feelings, the girl's anger subsided and she didn't say this again. Children often wrap up their feelings in physical aggression or verbal threats that involve excluding others from their play and activities (see p. 34). Being physically and/or verbally aggressive is what children at this stage of development know how to do. This will change with multiple problem-solving experiences, choices about inclusion, and repeated episodes of successful play with new friends.

## Stop, Think, & Discuss

*Think about your own friendships and how they developed. Why did you become friends with certain people? How much time did you spend together before you felt you were friends? How would you react if someone told you at a gathering of new people,* We are all friends here? *Does declaring it make it so? Discuss how and in what ways children form friendships.*

## What If...?

*Two children are arguing about who is going to put a block away. These little arguments happen all the time, and sometimes I find them very annoying, especially when we're in a hurry to finish cleaning up. Even when I give children a perfectly good solution to the problem, they still go on fighting. Why are children so picky about these little things? How can I put a stop to this kind of bickering behavior?*

# 12. Me Want To!

### A Typical Situation and Response...

### What Happened Here?

When the same type of problem happens often, the adult may feel impatient and try a "quick fix." However, there was a bigger issue for the children here than where to put the block: how control would be shared in their relationship. These children were trying to figure out what to say to "get their way" (assertiveness) and how to react to something different (compromise). This exploration will take multiple tries with *each and every relationship*. By taking sides and imposing a solution, the adult missed an opportunity to support relationship communication. This means there will very likely be more of these arguments in the future.

### If you find yourself in a situation like this, consider these strategies:

| INSTEAD OF... | TRY THIS... |
| --- | --- |
| Instead of assuming that older children should know better, | ► Understand that children of all ages continue to grow by solving big issues within these small episodes of conflict. |
| Instead of thinking you have to fix children's problems, | ► Enjoy the creativity, collaboration, and sense of confidence that emerges when children are put in charge of solving a problem. |

**What is the reason...**
**...to be patient as children figure out a solution? Sometimes it's difficult, particularly if children can't make a decision and we run out of time.**

In responding to children's problems, it's important to stay focused on your goals. Remind yourself why it is effective to ask children for solutions — they will learn communication skills, and you will not be problem-solving with them until they are adults! It's also important to remember that if we impose adult solutions to resolve children's problems, children will not have a chance to learn and practice the words and choices they need as problem solvers. They may become overly dependent on adults to provide solutions for them and may even come to feel resentful about their own lack of choice and control in situations that affect them.

Every new skill and every new friendship is built on a series of trial-and-error experiences. Each time there is enjoyment and success, relationships deepen and the skills that have worked become easier. As children practice negotiating with siblings, friends, and adults they come to learn that a friend is someone they know, like, and trust, and who is also willing to share control and decision-making with them. No amount of declaring *We're all friends here* will accomplish this. This type of learning, as important to success in life as math and reading, provides for the social growth and well-being that every parent and teacher wants for their children.

**A problem-solving response to the same situation:**

### What Happened Differently This Time?

The adult here did not see it as her job to "fix" the problem. Instead, she saw an opportunity to help strengthen the children's skills and their relationship by helping them negotiate a solution satisfactory to both. With this in mind, she labeled the situation as a *problem,* named feelings, held the contested object, restated the problem, and asked the children for solutions. Even when the children were unable to come up with a solution, the adult did not offer one. Instead, she gave them more time to try to think of a solution. When the children still did not offer an idea, the adult saw the chance to include another child in the process (skill-building for everyone!) This adult knew that supporting children to make choices motivates them (see p. 17) to stay engaged with the problem (i.e., in control).

Had the children not been able to think of something that worked for both of them, the adult could have said, *I have an idea. Do you want to hear my idea?* Asking this as a question allows the children to maintain control of the process. If children want to hear your idea, describe it to them. If they don't like it, ask them again, *Okay, then keep thinking — what can we do to solve it?* There is a very good chance that they will think of something.

### Something More to Consider...

It's essential that problem-solving language be clear and concrete. Each problem-solving situation will be slightly different. However, if adults consistently use the same words and phrases, children will become more consistent and empowered in their resolutions.

There are some important language guidelines to keep in mind. First, always start out by using the word *problem* to describe the situation. The statement *We have a problem* signals what will happen next, as children remember similar "problem" situations in which the adult listened to everyone involved and supported them in finding solutions. Second, name feelings (*You're both really mad*) rather than asking questions about feelings. This will help children to fully express feelings and begin to calm. Third, by saying *What can we do to solve this problem?* you let children know you have confidence in their ability to think of solutions. Respond to ideas that are unworkable with the phrase, *That's one idea...*, showing respect for every idea. Then add *Let's keep thinking of other ideas until we find one that works for everybody.* (Avoid asking *How can we make everyone happy?* — this is too difficult a goal). Finally, when children have agreed on a solution, instead of praising them by saying something like *Good job!* give specific encouragement by describing what worked: *You listened to each other, you both thought of ideas, and you solved the problem!*

### Stop, Think, & Discuss

*Think about a conflict you had with other adults. Discuss whether you were able to come up with a solution that worked for everyone yet allowed you to get your needs met. Did you get to practice this kind of problem solving when you were young? Most of us didn't, so we have to work harder to figure out how to "get our way" as we create collaborative solutions.*

# What If...?

*Very young children often argue about a little detail of their pretend play, like what time the sand cake will be done! How can the adult negotiate this kind of question, especially with very small children who do not yet grasp the meaning of time? How do you begin to problem-solve with children who are so young?*

## 13. *Not* Cake Time!

### A Typical Situation and Response...

### What Happened Here?

In this situation, the adult was watching the children play and had seen Rafi put sand in a pail. When Alice picked up this pail, announcing it was *cake time,* and Rafi angrily objected, the adult stepped in to "solve" the problem. Assuming the children were too young to negotiate, she forced Alice to give the pail back to Rafi and apologize to him. But with this solution, Rafi was treated as a victim who was helpless until the adult came along to rescue him. Alice was frustrated and took out her frustration on Rafi shortly thereafter. The adult's response created problems rather than solved them.

### If you find yourself in a situation like this, consider these strategies:

| INSTEAD OF... | TRY THIS... |
|---|---|
| Instead of assuming children are too young to negotiate and imposing a solution, | ► Simply describe what is happening from each child's perspective. |
| Instead of forcing children to say a fake *Sorry,* | ► Help them to resolve the problem in a way that results in genuine feelings about the solution: *Okay, cake time!. . .Hooray!* |

**What is the reason...**
**...to check in with both children about the solution and support what they decide, especially if one seems "dominating" and the other tends to give in more easily?**

As adults facilitate problem-solving, they will sometimes have concerns about the solution and whether it is fair to everyone involved. Negotiation, after all, is about balancing power. To empower children as they learn to solve problems, adults check in with children about what they want and what seems fair *to them.* To do otherwise is similar to taking a crayon and drawing for the child — it will not result in learning how to draw. We cannot force children to speak up, but we can give them openings. If one child offers something like *You can have it tomorrow!* and the other child does not protest, the adult might say, *Well, that's one idea. Let's keep thinking of ideas that give both of you a turn soon.* The phrase, *That's one idea...* shows acceptance of all ideas offered. *Let's keep thinking...* keeps the negotiation open. And *...ideas that will give both of you a turn soon,* makes the ultimate goal more clear. However, if the children do agree on an "unbalanced" or "unfair" solution, then support whatever they both clearly agree on. Sometimes children have to experience one-sidedness before they can learn to recognize it and create more balanced, fair-minded solutions.

#### A problem-solving response to the same situation:

### What Happened Differently This Time?

The adult in this actual situation began by having confidence that the children *could* negotiate even at this young age. She also began by listening very carefully to both children. Though Alice was very vocal, the adult made sure that Rafi had a chance to speak as well. The adult knew that if she "rescued" Rafi by speaking up for him, this would perpetuate his identity as Alice's victim. Once he was supported by the adult, Rafi assertively spoke up for himself — first saying *Cake time at two o'clock!* and then agreeing to an alternative time (*Yeah…three o'clock*) and to the choice of someone to announce it. At this young age, it is very important that Rafi has the chance to see himself as an active problem solver, rather than a passive victim.

The adult also recognized an opportunity for Alice to learn to be more accommodating of others through negotiation. When we respect children's ability to negotiate, no matter what their developmental level, children have a much more complex learning experience than if they're simply told, *Give it back — it's his!* The big difference here was that Alice had to stop her play, say *what* she wanted, listen to what Rafi wanted, agree on *when* and *how* "cake time" would happen, and then return to pretend play. That's a significant skill-building experience!

## Something More to Consider...

It will happen in every family and every classroom that the adult may be trying to sort out one conflict only to have others break out somewhere else. Don't despair! Let's consider how to manage keeping a cool head and a neutral attitude. Here are some strategies that will help on these demanding occasions.

First, if another conflict develops elsewhere while you're problem-solving with one group of children, say to the children you're with *I need to go talk to* ______. (If this first dispute is over toys, add *I'm going to keep this toy with me. I'll be right back.*) If the children want to come with you, that can work too. Second, if yet another conflict flares up, repeat the suggestions above and breathe! If you now have a small group of upset children around you, sit down with all of them, offering comfort and naming feelings in a calm voice. Name your feelings as well: *Wow, we're all feeling upset. Let's take a deep breath together, and then we'll sort out all these problems.* Lastly, return now to the details of each conflict until all the children have solutions. Finally, make a general statement to all the children about their problem-solving accomplishments, for example, *Phew! That was a lot of problem-solving, and we did it!!*

## Stop, Think, & Discuss

*Think about your own successes with problem-solving and consider ways to support the continuation of your problem-solving approach (such as posting the steps where they are easy to see). Describe your success stories to colleagues or family members, sharing what you have learned. Be prepared for skepticism, and know that you have chosen a positive path for young children with the biggest potential for long-term results!*

## What If...?

*One child bites another child. This behavior is one of the most difficult to witness and one of the hardest to stop. It's even more upsetting when the child who bites is older. Even if I react very firmly and clearly, and I isolate the child, I don't have much of an effect. Sometimes the child starts biting again as soon as I become distracted. Why do children do this? It's very hurtful and emotionally intense for everyone involved.*

# 14. Oww! He Bit Me!

### A Typical Situation and Response...

### What Happened Here?

The child in this situation is a four-year-old boy with a language delay, who has difficulty speaking and understanding others. Often, when he is not able to express what he wants, Luke becomes increasingly frustrated, and then he bites someone. The adult here, already frustrated herself by previous biting incidents involving Luke, responded first by trying to guess what he wanted and then by isolating him from the other children and adults. She thought this negative consequence — which she had used before — would motivate Luke to stop the hurtful behavior. However, this approach once again had no effect — he bit the next child who came nearby.

### If you find yourself in a situation like this, consider these strategies:

| INSTEAD OF... | TRY THIS... |
|---|---|
| Instead of assuming that the child is doing something "bad" and removing him, | ► Consider what the child might be trying to communicate with this "physical" behavior. |
| Instead of distancing a biting child from adults and other children, | ► Set clear limits and keep the child very near, enabling both close supervision and *more* attention rather than less. |

**What is the reason...**
**...to give children *more* attention when they have hurt someone?**
**Isn't this approach going to reward the *bad* behavior?**

First, it is important to understand that children bite for many reasons, but it is not because they are "bad" people. Some children are frustrated or afraid and express feelings orally — sucking on clothes, chewing on objects, and biting whenever they are upset or scared. Sometimes children between the ages of one and three bite as a way of expressing themselves because they do not yet have the words they need to communicate their thoughts and feelings. Older children may have more complicated emotional reasons for biting.

A child with challenging behaviors needs more attention because these behaviors are a physical expression of *unmet* needs (emotional, cognitive, or physical). When children do hurtful things and are isolated as a consequence, the child's needs become more desperate, and the behavior more intense. All children, particularly those with very strong needs, benefit most from positive attention. Neither punishment nor rewards are recommended by early childhood specialists as these responses will not meet children's needs or put an end to the behavior. To paraphrase educator Ross Greene (2005), if you swim out to a drowning child and hold up a dollar bill and yell, *Swim!* the child will drown. If he could swim (or speak), he would. It is important for adults to respond sensitively to children's cries for help, rather than ignoring or denying them.

**A problem-solving response to the same situation:**

### What Happened Differently This Time?

In this true situation (Dowling & Mitchell, 2007), Luke's teachers initially thought that because Luke's language delay inhibited his ability to communicate, he might be expressing himself physically — by biting — instead. Their hope was that as his language ability developed, his biting behavior would diminish, but this did not happen. Since Luke's random and repeated episodes of biting were not connected to a problem involving a particular child or toy, negotiation was not an appropriate response. The adults in Luke's life then looked at the situation from another angle. When a child bites, adults always physically intervene, briefly giving physical attention. However negative this attention may be, for some children it's better than no attention at all. As they considered this, the teachers also discovered that in his previous program, Luke had been told to hug the child he had bitten. Could Luke's biting behavior be his way of getting a hug?

The teachers began to offer Luke more hugs, more time on their laps, and more closely supervised inclusion. They frequently put an arm around him and gently stroked his back or arms. He responded to this approach very positively. It turned out that Luke was starving for *positive* physical attention, but previously that attention was focused on the child he had injured. Once the adults had understood and met Luke's physical and emotional needs positively, the children around him were happy to have him there, his language abilities began to improve, and within two weeks the biting behavior stopped.

## Something More to Consider...

Though the biting behavior illustrated here with an older child is somewhat unusual, it is important to recognize that biting is a fairly common behavior among toddlers and even young three-year-olds — in fact, for any child functioning at that age level, it is a *predictable* developmental behavior. Knowing this, parents and teachers need to be prepared when biting occurs and not overreact. Overreaction may actually increase the child's interest in chomping down on innocent bystanders. Stay calm, set limits firmly (e.g., *Biting must stop*), and find a way to "shadow" the child who is biting so that you can intervene before it happens again and becomes a "successful" strategy for the child. It should be expected that young children are going to bite more often when they are tired, hungry, stressed, and/or needing attention.

Avoid drastic measures like isolation, biting back, or other punishments. None of these have been found to work. Parents and teachers of children who bite must try to avoid feeling embarrassed that they have failed somehow. Shake off the disapproving looks from others and be secure in the knowledge that biting is as common as nose-picking, wall-scribbling, and soggy pants. With some time, positive support for your child, and a sense of humor, this too will pass.

## Stop, Think, & Discuss

*Adults often respond to children's hurtful behaviors by hurting them: washing their mouths out with soap, spanking them, and/or forcibly removing children for a time-out. Discuss the possibility that these reactions are an outlet for adult frustration, as they certainly don't teach children problem-solving skills. Instead, they reinforce physical aggression. Children learn what adults model. Shouldn't we try to model compassion?*

## What If...?

*There are times when children refuse to do the "everyday" things that I ask of them — things they have to do, such as going inside for lunch. Sometimes they simply refuse to do what I say and even talk back to me. It's disrespectful and it really bothers me when I can't get them to behave. How can I make my children be more respectful and listen to me — they really are not good listeners.*

# 15. We Don't Want To!

### A Typical Situation and Response...

### What Happened Here?

This adult seemed to think that being a "good" parent or teacher meant commanding instant control of children. Victor didn't immediately "obey" and complained about the adult's request. The adult interpreted his tone and his answer (*We don't want to go in*) as disrespectful "back talk." It really was simply an expression of Victor's feelings. The adult's response (*You're being a bad boy*) escalated the situation into a contest of wills and "winning." Notice how the child's body language and tone (frame 3) mimics the adult's authoritative stance (frame 2). The adult did not listen to Victor, and in turn, Victor did not listen to the adult.

### If you find yourself in a situation like this, consider these strategies:

| INSTEAD OF... | TRY THIS... |
|---|---|
| Instead of expecting children to "obey" instantly when we ask them to stop having fun, | ► Give them extra time to adjust to the idea with a warning. Explain your request so that children can understand it. |
| Instead of mistaking children's refusals as "back talk," | ► Don't take the behavior personally (which may be hard!). Children's refusals reflect their desire to continue their fun. There is no conscious intention to be disrespectful. |

**What is the reason...**
**...children seem to be such poor listeners?**

Young children can be very good and enthusiastic listeners, as long as they have adequate time to respond to what they hear and what they hear is mostly positive. Children need 20–60 seconds to fully process an adult's request and answer thoughtfully. If they are not given enough time to absorb and understand what has been said, they may react with frustration. Also, if the talk they hear is often negative, filled with lots of *Nos*, children's frustration will likely turn to anger. Adults can easily mistake refusals as "back talk" or "bad" behavior, when often it is simply surprise, frustration, or self-protective "tuning out." If a child initially says *No* in response to an adult's request, it is clear that the child has "listened" but didn't like what he or she heard and openly said so! It might be useful to admire this as assertiveness and work *with* it, rather than discourage it.

Respect for children's needs will generate respect for adult's requests. Cooperation is more likely if the adult offers an explanation (rather than bribes or threats) and limited choices (e.g., *Your choices now are to hold Ashley's hand or hold mine*). Limiting the choices to two makes it easier for a child who is upset to negotiate. Children learn to be more effective listeners from those who listen effectively to them.

**A problem-solving response to the same situation:**

## What Happened Differently This Time?

In this response, the adult had already listened to the children and they had agreed on five more minutes of play, using the large homemade salt timer (see Appendix for instructions). The timer made the passing of time very visual, helping the children to actually "see" five minutes and to understand how long they had left to play. The adult's warning and explanation of what was going to happen next gave the children a few minutes to adjust to the idea of stopping play and going into lunch. However, even with support, children may still have a difficult time stopping play, as Victor did. The adult took the approach of being positive and respectful (*You're having a lot of fun out here with the trucks and sand.... I know you're disappointed*). A pause here helped Victor absorb the fact that the adult understood his dilemma. The adult then calmly restated that Victor needed to choose *how* he would go inside, not *if* he would go.

In this situation, even though Victor's enthusiasm was acknowledged, his upset feelings continued. Being clear and giving limited choices (*Staying out is not a choice right now. Your choices are...*) proved to be very effective. By giving Victor two choices *You need to choose or I'll need to choose for you. I think you'll feel better if* you *choose,* the adult demonstrated respect for Victor's abilities and emerging independence while not overwhelming him with options.

### Something More to Consider...

Solving problems that happen around routines and transitions require special consideration by parents and teachers. However, if a pattern of resistance to a regular routine develops, consider doing group or family problem-solving. First, consider those times of the day (e.g., toileting, preparing for nap, getting dressed, etc.) that have become problematic on a regular basis. Observe carefully at these times, noticing the children's behavior and your own reactions. Later, when everyone involved is calm and the problem is not happening, sit down together, either eating a simple snack or playing with toys, and discuss the problem.

Before gathering family members or small groups in a classroom, think through how you can positively present the problem to be discussed. State the problem clearly, without blaming. For example, you might say *Sometimes when it's time for lunch, it's hard to stop playing. What can we do so that getting to lunch is easier and more fun? Does anyone have any ideas?* Phrasing the question in this way will help motivate children to think of ideas, since having fun is a major goal for them. Be sure to listen to and respect *all* ideas, even if they seem silly or unrealistic. Think of the negotiation as "practice" at coming up with solutions for problems. Chances are that the discussion alone and the confidence you've shown in children's solutions, however simple, will generate more cooperation.

### Stop, Think, & Discuss

*Think about daily transitions and discuss signaling these times with a chime or bells, and using a timer. Also, discuss the ratio of negative to positive words children hear in a day. Agree to avoid labels that are disrespectful of children. Set a goal of communicating with positive expectations and choices that empower children and encourage listening. (See Appendix for more on timers, p. 93.)*

## What If...?

*A child pushes another child, out of the blue, for no reason! It sometimes seems as if some children enjoy annoying others. I don't want to use time-outs, but I don't think it's safe for children like this to be around other children — I'm just never sure what's going to set them off. What do I do to keep everyone safe?*

# 16. I Hate Myself!

### A Typical Situation and Response...

### What Happened Here?

Frustrated and concerned about children's safety, the adult here "lost her cool" and immediately removed the aggressive child without really thinking about the child's needs. She imposed a complicated solution — *Read a book, calm down, and stay away...* — without trying to see the situation from the child's point of view. Though the adult didn't call her "solution" a *time-out,* it was. By expecting Tahkia, who was already upset, to manage so many directives as well as isolation, the adult set her up for failure. This could easily become a negative cycle for Tahkia; without adult help, she may not be able to find her way out of it.

### If you find yourself in a situation like this, consider these strategies:

| INSTEAD OF... | TRY THIS... |
|---|---|
| Instead of showing your frustration, | ► Prepare yourself to *appear* calm by using a calm voice, getting on the children's level and naming feelings. |
| Instead of perpetuating negative cycles, | ► Stop the behavior and give follow-up support with problem solving. |
| Instead of removing children from the social situation, | ► Encourage them to listen to others' feelings and to express their needs in a different way. |

### What is the reason...
### ...to problem-solve and give attention to a child who has just hurt someone?

Children's challenging behaviors always happen for a reason — prompted by a conscious or unconscious goal or desire. In this situation, Tahkia clearly was a child with urgent, unmet needs, but she was not consciously aware of this. It is highly likely that a child's hit, bite, or insult indicates a need for attention. For children who have intense needs, negative attention is often better than no attention. Sometimes adults consider this behavior to be manipulative on the child's part. However, this assessment is unfair to children who do not yet have the verbal ability to communicate their needs clearly. To be manipulative also requires an understanding of actions, emotions, and consequences which is cognitively beyond most preschoolers' level of conscious thinking. It is not likely that you will hear a preschool child say, *Excuse me, but I really hurt inside and I need someone to spend some quality time with me.* Instead, some children may say, *I hate myself* — a clear indication of emotional pain. We need to give children comfort and understanding (e.g., *You're really upset with yourself*) and the positive attention they sometimes desperately need. Such positive moments offered by the adult will develop trust between adult and child. In time, children will learn to *ask* for what they need: *Will you play with me?*

**A problem-solving response to the same situation:**

## What Happened Differently This Time?

In this alternative response, the adult immediately recognized Tahkia's neediness and low self-esteem, using the word *problem* to let Tahkia know she wanted to talk to her, not yell or punish. This helped Tahkia trust that she would be safe, and she stopped the negative behavior. The adult then called to Fari with the goal of supporting what each child needed: limit-setting and positive attention for Tahkia and support for Fari to speak up. Tahkia struggled anxiously (laughing after doing something hurtful is a sure sign of nervousness in children). The adult set limits and named feelings and then quickly moved on to engaging both children in a resolution. Still agitated, Tahkia agreed to talk, but she was clearly upset with herself. The adult turned to Fari suggesting he say, *Please don't push me and don't call me stupid* (rather than something like, *I don't like that,* which can provoke an angry response). This was respectful and clear. Tahkia answered *Okay.* The adult then turned to Tahkia and stated her concerns using "*I*" statements (e.g., *I'm worried about…*). While avoiding blame (something needy children *don't* need), the adult asked Tahkia to solve the problem. This opened the door for Tahkia to ask, constructively, for the attention she sorely needed. Her emerging ability to ask for, rather than show, her need for attention was directly linked to her trust in the adult's positive support.

### Something More to Consider...

Once the conflict between the two children in the problem-solving situation was resolved, the remaining issue was how to support the child who had pushed, laughed about it, and said *I hate myself.* Since children may not always know or be able to explain *why* they are upset, the adult did not ask Tahkia questions but instead made a clear "I" statement to express her concerns (e.g., *I'm feeling worried about...*) and then stated the specific behaviors she was worried *about*. The adult's statement, *I'm feeling worried about pushing and about how upset you are with yourself,* did not blame the child or ask questions about feelings Tahkia couldn't answer. The statement also did not try to deny the child's negative feelings about herself. It is important to simply name and accept how badly a child is feeling so that he or she knows the adult is truly listening. This acceptance provides safety, and the discussion remains concrete: *How can we play so we're all safe?* This question enabled Tahkia to say *what* she needed even though she probably could not say *why* she felt so negatively about herself. By practicing how to ask for what she needed, rather than getting attention with negative behavior, Tahkia came to understand how to get her needs met without hurting others.

### Stop, Think, & Discuss

*Think about real jobs you can give children that will build self-esteem, such as asking them to be problem solvers (calling on them for help with solutions to conflicts), puzzle or tape "experts" (referring other children to them for help), or leaders during large-group activities. Real work and responsibility give children positive ways to contribute and strengthen self-confidence, hopefully changing the negative image of how they see themselves.*

## What If...?

*My child has been having trouble at day care. Before pickup time, I get really anxious about the awful things I'm going to hear from the teachers when I get there. I understand that teachers get frustrated when children don't behave, and they feel they have to talk to parents about what's going on, but it seems unfair for teachers to focus on only the negative things that have happened during the day. What's the best way for teachers and parents to talk about a child's challenging behaviors?*

# 17. It Was a Bad Day!

### A Typical Situation and Response...

### What Happened Here?

Frustrated with Tahkia's behavior, the teacher "emptied out" her frustrations on the parent (*...bad day! She did a lot of pushing and name-calling*). This description made it sound like the hurting happened *all day!* If Tahkia repeatedly hears such negative descriptions of herself, she will be more likely to fulfill the negative behavior expected of her. It was also hard for Tahkia's parent to hear the teacher's discouraging description of the day. The parent reacted by piling on punitive consequences that Tahkia would have to face at home, when the problem really needed to be resolved at school.

### If you find yourself in a situation like this, consider these strategies:

| INSTEAD OF... | TRY THIS... |
| --- | --- |
| Instead of parents and teachers thinking of a day as *good* or *bad*, | ► Parents can ask questions about their child's day, and teachers can give nonjudgmental descriptions of successful and challenging events, emphasizing the learning that happened. |
| Instead of describing an incident by focusing on a child's hurtful behavior, | ► Describe what the child did to help solve the problem. |

**What is the reason...**
**...to avoid negative descriptions of children's actions and behaviors?**
**What are some other ways to talk about them?**

Parents and teachers can easily lose track of a child's growth and progress when that child is experiencing difficulties. If parent-teacher conversations about the day focus only on the negatives, these exchanges can get bogged down in resentment, blame, and a poor attitude toward the child (who is already challenged enough!). A discouraging report may also get children into even more trouble at home.

What might parents and teachers say to one another so that conflicts become considered rich learning moments? If parents ask teachers *Was it a good day or a bad day?* teachers might say something like *I'm not really comfortable describing the day in general terms — there were so many things that happened that show your child is learning new things! Let me tell you about her block building and a problem she solved....* Conversely, if teachers say, *Your child had a bad day...*, parents might respond by saying *It helps me and my child when we avoid talking about the day using terms like* good and bad. *Can we talk about what happened and how my child was supported to resolve any problems?* Parents can then discuss issues further with their child at home by saying something like *I heard that you solved a problem at school today.* Resist the urge to lecture, and just listen.

**A problem-solving response to the same situation:**

## What Happened Differently This Time?

In this situation, both the parent and the teacher took a positive and detailed approach to talking about the events of the day, each helping to set a concerned but optimistic tone. The teacher gave the parent time to fully greet her child and enjoy that special moment of reuniting. When asking about the day, the parent posed a specific question: *What kinds of things did Tahkia do today?* This made it much easier for the teacher to share details, rather than make judgments about the day. Tahkia had a busy day, filled with all kinds of learning experiences, including problem solving with another child. The teacher shared details about the dinosaur house, keeping the more challenging moments in perspective. The teacher knew the parent well enough to know that she wouldn't overreact by saying things like *I told you to be good. No TV and a spanking for you!* The teacher also waited until the child was out of earshot and then shared some details of how the problem was worked out. Knowing that children's social mistakes are just one more area of learning, the parent and teacher shared how that learning was progressing. Tahkia's mistake wasn't an end point, it was a beginning.

## Something More to Consider...

It is very common for parents and teachers to talk about children as if they were not there. Imagine for a moment that you are standing in a grocery line next to two people you know and they begin to talk about a mistake you made, but nothing about the positive way the situation was resolved. Imagine on top of that you had your mouth full of dental gauze and were unable to speak up for yourself — and besides they were bigger than you and they looked angry! No doubt you would feel frustrated and belittled, and you might begin to wonder if you really were as horrible as they said. Children feel this too — the difference is that they easily believe that what is being said about them is *true*. Hearing lots of negatives may discourage children's ability to think positively about themselves. For many children who live with constant disapproval, it is easier to get an angry or frustrated response rather than positive attention from adults, and a vicious cycle begins. It's important for parents and teachers to think about *when* they give their children the most attention — when children are doing something "annoying" or when they are constructively engaged and undemanding. Join children's play when it is constructive. Participating in play, even for a few minutes, encourages positive behaviors. When conflicts arise, problem-solve and then be forgiving of mistakes, and children will rise to those positive thoughts.

## Stop, Think, & Discuss

*Consider strategies for supporting positive behaviors without using reward systems (which create dependence and weaken self-esteem). Put up drawings and photos of things children have done and/or write down their stories of a helpful task or a creative solution to a problem. Help children recall the day during mealtimes or while you play together, focusing on positive events and details. Notice what kind of encouragement works well with your individual children.*

## What If...?

*Two children of very different ages start arguing, and the older, more verbal child comes up with a one-sided solution that works just for her. Shouldn't I give these children ideas for a solution that's fair to both of them, especially when only one child is able to talk? I'm really not at all sure that my children, even the older one, can come up with good solutions. Often when I ask for ideas, they don't say anything, or simply state again what they want. How do I help them to come up with ideas?*

# 18. No Fair!

### A Typical Situation and Response...

### What Happened Here?

The adult decided that the younger child needed someone to step in for her so that she would be assured a turn on the horse. The adult insisted that as a "big girl," the older child should give the younger one a turn. Hearing the adult was on her side, the younger child may have concluded that yelling *Meee!* louder was an effective strategy! Unfortunately, she continued to use this tactic when the adult was not nearby. Since the adult missed the opportunity to try a new way to respond to this conflict using children's ideas, the yelling continued next time.

### If you find yourself in a situation like this, consider these strategies:

| INSTEAD OF... | TRY THIS... |
| --- | --- |
| Instead of thinking that children are *too young,* have too little language, or are too egocentric to problem-solve, | ► Ask them for solutions, being optimistic and pausing for a minute or two, and giving both children time to think of ideas. |
| Instead of assuming that children know the specifics of what they will do when they decide to *share,* | ► Ask children *What will you each be doing when you share?* |

**What is the reason...**
**...to give time to child-made solutions, and how do you do it?**

Here are a few basic tips: First, pose *What...?* questions that keep the focus on solving the problem concretely. For example, after restating the problem, ask *What can we do to solve this problem?* Avoid *How can we make you both happy?* This is too abstract. Second, give children time to answer the question. Wait patiently, or say *Hmmm...we need to think hard about what will work....* Avoid *Why...?* questions like *Why aren't you sharing?* — they are accusatory and put blame on children. Next, if there are still no mutually agreed-on ideas, or time is short, ask other children for an idea. Children often like ideas offered by peers. Finally, if you have tried all of the above, you can encourage children to decide on solutions by saying *I have an idea. Do you want to hear my idea?* However, those involved in the conflict get to choose the solution, even if the idea was yours or someone else's.

Sometimes a child will walk away saying *He can have it...I don't care.* The adult can respond, *That's one idea. We could give it to him, or we can keep thinking of ideas that give you both a turn.* As children offer ideas, check in to make sure the idea is okay with everyone. A collaborative, child-made solution is one of the great gifts of problem solving.

#### A problem-solving response to the same situation:

### What Happened Differently This Time?

Even the very young child of 18 months old here showed that she was capable of understanding how to problem-solve. This happened because of the adult's patience and confidence in both of the children's abilities. The adult here also knew that the older child would become even more upset if she put her hand on the horse to stop the rocking while they talked. Though this strategy would be something to consider in many situations, in some cases it is helpful to give children some space for a moment, as happened here. It can also work well for *everyone* to hold a disputed object together (very young children may think they are losing the toy when the adult holds it). In this situation, the adult described the problem from nearby, and waited…confident that the older child (and maybe even the younger one!) would think of a solution. It took the older child a minute or two to come up with an idea. Because she was given this chance to choose a solution and, most importantly, the time to do it, she did choose one — the timer! The timer was a brilliant idea for a toddler — it's big and concrete and fun to watch. After a few repetitions of this kind of solution, the toddler began to enjoy the kind of control it gave her, and she was able to do it independently later on.

## Something More to Consider...

Children who are forced to "share" may learn the *mechanics* of sharing — learning how to divide materials or use time intervals to measure turns — but they are not truly *sharing*. Real sharing requires a *desire* to share on the part of the children involved. To nurture this desire, adults can give children a chance to negotiate and make choices about the details of what they will actually do when they are *sharing*.

Even when a child refuses to problem-solve at all, adults can point out the choices that remain. Gently tell that child that he or she can come up with a solution or you and the *other children* will need to decide on one. Be sure to use a nonthreatening tone of voice and then re-invite the child to participate in creating a solution.

When children offer vague solutions like *We can share* or *We can take turns*, it's important to understand that children have different interpretations about what those suggestions mean. One child may think *sharing* means *I'll have it now, you'll have it tomorrow* while another child assumes *We'll both use it together* or *We'll trade it back and forth*. For this reason, it's helpful to ask, *When you share, what will you each be doing?* or *When you take turns, what will that look like?* The mediator's job is to help children be clear about what they are agreeing to and how it will work, *exactly*.

## Stop, Think, & Discuss

*Though optimal learning happens for children during actual conflicts, adults can also think about proactive ways to support children's solutions. Do you have books that illustrate social problem solving? How about a puppet show that dramatizes a conflict? Get the puppet conflict started, then pause and ask your children,* What do you think they can do to solve the problem? I know you have lots of ideas.

## What If...?

*Two older children often get into a fight over a toy, and they both say they had it first. Sometimes they accuse each other of lying or say something insulting. It's not always clear what has happened, and so many issues come up that I don't know what to address first. I tell children to say* I'm sorry, *and sometimes I even suggest a solution, but it doesn't seem to matter — one child usually ends up unhappy, and the problem doesn't get solved. Shouldn't the older preschoolers, who have become more experienced problem solvers, be able to solve problems on their own?*

# 19. I Have an Idea!

### A Typical Situation and Response...

### What Happened Here?

The adult here made a snap judgment about who was right and tried to quickly "fix" the situation, forgetting that these children were experienced problem solvers who may have needed a minute to remember to use their negotiating skills. The adult made an assumption that the child whose hands were on the block was the one who had it first (not so fast — there are often other factors). She told the other child to apologize and then decided on the solution for both of them. Because the adult took sides, one child received no support and rather than remembering to problem-solve, that child became more angry and frustrated. Though this child obeyed and said *Sorry!*, it is easy to see that there was little feeling behind his apology!

### If you find yourself in a situation like this, consider these strategies:

| INSTEAD OF... | TRY THIS... |
| --- | --- |
| Instead of jumping to conclusions, | ► Remain neutral, listen to what children are saying, and repeat it back. |
| Instead of demanding that children say *I'm sorry* or imposing a solution, | ► Support the children involved in creating their own solution. |

**What is the reason...**
**...that telling children to say *I'm sorry* is not recommended?**

As we think about this question, it will help to recognize first that *sorry* is a word that describes a feeling. The complete sentence for this is *I feel sorry*. But can we demand that children have a particular feeling? Children can't *feel* regret if they haven't had a chance to understand the problem. They may not yet be capable of feeling empathy for the hurt they have caused someone else. The phrase likely has no internal meaning for them. If we ask children to say *I'm sorry* and they don't actually *feel* sorry, then we are essentially asking children to lie.

Adults may think that forcing children to say *I'm sorry* is a way to resolve problems or to teach children manners. First, since nothing about the situation has actually changed or been resolved, this is confusing to children. The feelings and the problem still exist, so saying *sorry* is merely a Band-Aid on the situation. (Some children may even end up thinking *I can do whatever I want — hit or grab — and then just say* I'm sorry, *and the adult will leave me alone!*) Furthermore, a forced apology is not evidence of manners; it's an indication that the child has obeyed the adult's direction, but obedience does not create resolution. The child forced to say a fake *I'm sorry* may hold onto unresolved anger, and the problem will likely recur.

**A problem-solving response to the same situation:**

### What Happened Differently This Time?

In this true situation, the adult took a few seconds to observe as she moved closer to the children. Knowing that even experienced problem-solvers sometimes need help getting started, she quickly got down on their level and put her hands on the block they both wanted. The children immediately knew that she was not going to take sides and that they would both receive support. As the adult named their feelings, she also repeated back that each was saying they had it "first." (See #9 for more on why children say *I had it first.*) It is important to say, *You're both saying you had it first…* so that the children know that you are really listening. If you don't do this, they will likely keep repeating *But I had it first!* The adult set limits on the name-calling but understood that simply stopping hurtful behaviors was not a resolution. She continued, *So you both need a lot [of blocks]…What can we do to solve this?* With the problem clearly identified, the children's negotiating skills kicked in — empowered by the adult to make choices about the solution, the children agreed on the truly remarkable idea of drawing the blocks and counting together how many were needed, and then Abby asked for a photo of the buildings they made *from our problem.*

## Something More to Consider...

Without conflict resolution support, children may use their creative energy on increasingly harsh language as they try to express their needs and wants. With adult support, however, they become more experienced problem solvers, using that maturing creative energy to decide on collaborative and inventive social solutions.

Indeed, as adults mediate with children, they will observe many delightful changes. Children begin to calm and find solutions much more quickly, and they gradually come to need less and less adult help negotiating (see #21). Children come to understand that it is their responsibility to find a solution that works for everyone, and their ability to think imaginatively becomes quite striking, as we see here with Abby and Abram's agreement to draw their buildings as part of the solution. Children who have had lots of practice at creating solutions really do enjoy this part! As children's skills mature, they begin to bring their full potential to the effort, agreeing on increasingly cooperative and complicated solutions. In this true situation, Abby and Abram, both capable of detailed drawings, really enjoyed putting their building ideas on paper and resolving the number question this way. As a result of this and subsequent problem-solving experiences, their skills became evident to the other children who would call on them during a conflict. They willingly came forward to help, occasionally mediating entirely on their own.

### Stop, Think, & Discuss

*Think about one or two children whose problem-solving skills developed, as they learned to solve problems by staying calm, using their verbal abilities, and listening more carefully to the ideas of others. Also, think about an inventive solution created by children that surprised you. Discuss how these experiences are changing your relationships with children, and how problem solving is changing your feelings about being a successful parent or teacher.*

## What If...?

*My children fight over everyday items like stuffed animals, a favorite cup, a cherished chair. Do I need to problem-solve with them even when these kinds of conflict occur? Are there any conflicts that don't call for a problem-solving approach? Sometimes I'm in a hurry and I just want the children to go to sleep or sit down and eat! Often I don't feel I have the time (or, to be honest, the patience) to engage in a full negotiation.*

# 20. We Solved It!

### A Typical Situation and Response...

### What Happened Here?

The adult did not seem to recognize that this typical "everyday" conflict and interaction provided an opportunity for the children to learn about problem solving. Instead, the adult avoided engaging with the children, focusing on who had the toy first and using the "fix-it" approach, siding with one child. This *avoidance* (of problem-solving) approach reinforced for the children that yelling *I had it first!* worked. So the next day, when the conflict occurred again, the children still lacked problem-solving skills and the hurting got worse. Soon the adult will discover that even the threat of throwing the stuffed animal away will not solve the problem.

### If you find yourself in a situation like this, consider these strategies:

| INSTEAD OF... | TRY THIS... |
|---|---|
| Instead of avoiding the conflict by "fixing" the problem with a command, | ► Calmly state that there is a problem, set limits, and hold the object in dispute. |
| Instead of taking sides and missing an opportunity to build children's skills, | ► Support children's emerging skills, and stay neutrally close by as they solve the problem. |

**What is the reason...**
**...to stop hurtful behaviors without yelling *No!!*?**

There will be times, of course, that worried adults will yell *No* or *Stop* to children, especially in dangerous situations. There will also be occasions when the adult really will need to say, *Stop. We don't have time to talk. Here are your choices for right now. Later we can problem-solve.* It's important that the adult follow through with this promise and check in later to see if there is still a problem to be solved.

When setting limits as problem-solving begins, adults can be most effective by stating clearly what they *do* want to have happen. Instead of saying *No,* Josh, the adult in the problem-solving scenario (see next page) said calmly and clearly, *Name-calling and yelling must stop.* Because Josh described the offending *actions* right away, the children understood what needed to stop. If adults simply yell *No,* children may become frightened and confused, wondering what the adult is saying *No* to. This resulting fear and confusion can even intensify children's hurtful behaviors.

Josh's simple, direct statement let the children know that he was not angry at *them* or *their feelings,* but rather was concerned about the specific *actions* of *yelling* and *name-calling.* As a result, these behaviors stopped. Adults can use this strategy to respond to a range of challenging behaviors (biting, spitting, hitting, etc.). Once limits have been set and heard, problem-solving can begin.

**A problem-solving response to the same situation:**

## What Happened Differently This Time?

The children in this true story had experienced many problem-solving negotiations with Josh and trusted him completely. Rather than feeling threatened or blamed by him, the children heard the word *problem,* and they knew what to do next. Josh calmly told them that he would hold the contested object, and he set limits on the yelling and name-calling. He then sat down with the dog and watched as the children negotiated on their own to find a solution (i.e., Kaylani stated, *We have to solve the problem.*) Their negotiation was very lively (with even more give-and -take exchanges than could be captured in the illustration), and both children had ideas about what to do. The adult's role was to provide neutral supervision, ensuring the children's safety and waiting patiently, confident the children would find a solution agreeable to both. Interestingly, the children's problem-solving involved a choice between instant gratification (get the dog today) and delayed gratification (get the dog tomorrow and for six sleeps), which gave them a chance to ponder a problem often encountered in life. In deciding who would have the dog now or later, the children had to think through what each option had to offer. The difference between an adult-imposed solution and a remarkably unique child-made solution is the difference between confused obedience versus the challenge of cause-and-effect thinking and respectful negotiation that builds life skills.

## Something More to Consider...

Consider how you use your adult power or authority: Do you like to have all the answers? Come up with the perfect solution? Get problem situations fixed quickly? If so, ask yourself this: *How will children learn to solve problems if adults keep providing them with solutions?* We constantly need to ask ourselves what is most important: Is it what *we* think is the best way to solve a problem or how we can best support children to solve problems themselves so that they learn new communication skills?

Once you have decided to empower children to recognize and solve problems, there is an easy strategy for using your power neutrally: *pretend that you are clueless.* Do this by saying something like *Oh, I don't know what happened. Can you tell me? I'll hold this while we talk. You can each tell your story about the problem, and then we'll see what ideas you have to solve it.* As for the question of whether you should problem-solve every time there is a conflict, consider problem-solving whenever children are hurtful and are in need of a new skill — in other words, yes. Problem-solve every challenging behavior you encounter. Once we empower children, we too will be sitting neutrally nearby while they negotiate *on their own.*

## Stop, Think, & Discuss

*There are two typical adult responses to conflicts: authoritarian and avoidance-driven. Discuss which response you experienced as a child. Did adults tell you what to do? Or did they avoid conflict (e.g., by saying* Be nice*)? This past experience may help to explain your "gut" reaction to conflicts as an adult. Think of the first words you say in response to a conflict, and then consider how you might change them.*

## What If...?

*Children begin arguing and yelling at each other and I'm not sure if I should intervene. Even though they have had lots of problem-solving experience, I worry when there's a conflict between children of different ages and abilities, especially if a younger child is involved. I also have trouble not interfering with their solution if I think there is a "better" way for them to work out the problem. When is it appropriate to let children problem-solve without any help at all?*

# 21. This Is a Problem.

### A Child-Mediated Situation and Response...

### What Happened Here?

Three children, two four-year-olds and five-year-old Abby (the same girl as in #19), were building ramps for rolling tennis balls. Three-year-old Atticus, who has a language delay, approached and picked up a ramp. The older children all yelled *No!* but the shouting ended quickly. (Sometimes it can take a few minutes for children's problem-solving skills to kick in.) Adults saw no reason to intervene. Abby quickly spoke to Atticus in a way that she knew would work with him. She signed *No* and said, *This is a problem.* Abby recognized that the developing situation was a "problem" and trusted the process that would follow.

### If you find yourself in a situation like this, consider these strategies:

| INSTEAD OF... | TRY THIS... |
|---|---|
| Instead of assuming that arguing children need an adult mediator, | ► Observe for a moment, remaining calm and hopeful. |
| Instead of intervening with *your* solution, | ► Extend confidence to children by encouraging *their* ideas, rather than intervening when their solutions are not as "perfect" as you would like. |

Continued on next page

**What is the reason...**
**...that children experienced in problem solving willingly engage in the process on some days, yet may have a hard time doing it on other days?**

Children who know how to problem-solve, or those who are just learning, may sometimes refuse to negotiate, and they should not be forced. They may be feeling ill, scared, agitated, or simply lacking the necessary energy.

When children refuse or forget to engage in problem solving during a conflict that involves them directly, begin problem-solving as always by approaching the child calmly and naming feelings. Then ask, *What's the problem?* Sometimes hearing the word problem is enough to trigger the process. However, if a child is silent or says, *I don't want to talk about it,* name feelings again: *You're upset — it seems like you don't want to talk about it.* If you still get no response, say something like *It seems that you don't want to problem-solve. I want you to know that this means that we* [you and whoever else is involved] *will decide on a solution, and then we will tell you.* Still no response? Calmly continue: *So your choices now are to problem-solve with us now or, in a few minutes, we will tell you our solution and what you will need to do. Which do you want to choose?* If the child still refuses, be respectful, and hope that next time he or she will choose to problem-solve.

## A Child-Mediated Situation and Response (continued)

### What Happened Differently This Time?

Because this was an independent, child-mediated negotiation, several things happened differently:

First, since Abby was an experienced problem-solver, the children respected her skills and followed her lead. As soon as she said, *Atticus wants to play,* the two other children willingly shared: *Here's how you do it, Atticus.* (Children teaching children is such an important benefit of mixed-age groupings in classrooms and homes). Second, when Atticus pulled apart the ramps for the second time, one of the boys used the same approach that Abby had just modeled. He signed *No* and said, *No, Atticus…this is a problem.* And last, Abby modeled another critical problem-solving skill. She restated the problem to the older boys: *He wants to use the ramps you have, but he doesn't have the same words as us.* Then, she restated the problem to Atticus, describing it from his perspective: *They are using those and you want them.* One of the boys immediately responded to the opportunity Abby so eloquently clarified for him — he offered all the ramps to Atticus and said, *He can use them!* It is possible that not wanting to play cooperatively with a less verbal child might have been why the boys moved on (though Atticus was a popular playmate), or perhaps they were simply more interested in other building materials. Their reasons don't matter as long as the solution was their choice and worked for everyone.

## Something More to Consider...

Sometimes children who are very experienced problem solvers will suddenly appear to be bored or annoyed with the adult-mediated process. This attitude might indicate a need for more independence, and it is a sign that it is time to encourage children to become independent mediators within the home or classroom. Sit down as a group with your family or class and discuss this possibility. If children agree that they would like to choose times to take on this role, discuss the details of how it would work.

Here is an example of how one group of preschool children and adults set up this process: At a meeting that included all the teachers and children in the classroom, everyone agreed that the children could choose to be problem-solvers or mediators for the day. Everyone else in the group agreed that they would be respectful and cooperate with the peer "Problem Solver." The group also agreed on a set of four simplified steps, written in words and symbols on a clipboard, that could be "read" by even the youngest five-year-old. After several role-play practice sessions, the job of Problem Solver was rotated among those who wanted the job. At first, an adult was available to give support, reminding the new mediators what to do when they got stuck. Soon however, they were managing on their own. Pause and imagine your children as mediators. And then imagine the global possibilities.

## Stop, Think, & Discuss

*Even when problem solving is used often, there will still be conflicts and differences to sort out. This is simply the nature of life. Think about intense conflicts, and their likely causes, that occur repeatedly in your home or classroom. As parents and teachers, we need to engage in ongoing discussions, adjusting how we support our children through the next stage of growth in their young lives.*

# Conclusion

In the final scenario, Abby was focused on helping Atticus and the two boys succeed in their play. Using her problem-solving skills, she had gone beyond the egocentric approach more typical of preschoolers in order to focus on the needs of others. And, as a mediator, she had accomplished astonishing success at the same time for herself. Children may not engage in such eager negotiation every day, but as they experience success, it will happen more and more often. Over time, young children's challenging behaviors will be replaced by increasingly frequent moments of creative and productive collaboration. It is how a new approach to the strong emotions and conflicts of life will happen — one negotiation and one child at a time.

The parents and teachers of Abby, Atticus, and the two other boys in this true final story, as well as adults everywhere who support children, all deserve a huge round of applause for the skills that they have inspired, modeled, and nurtured for those children in their care. Supporting the social-emotional growth and intelligence demonstrated here requires patience, respect, and a consistent belief in children and their emerging abilities.

The children in all the real problem-solving experiences illustrated here have demonstrated in conflict after conflict that negotiation can be a lively give-and-take learning process. It requires that each of the children listen to each other as they look beyond their own egocentric needs and figure out what will

*Using her problem-solving skills, 5-year-old mediator Abby helped other children, including Atticus (above), succeed at their play.*

work for all of them. Having an adult nearby as a reminder of what they need to do will eventually be *all they need* at a certain stage in their problem-solving learning. As their confidence builds, soon they will be ready to problem-solve, or even mediate, independently.

*Atticus successfully rolls the ball down the ramp.*

As children and adults learn to negotiate together, there will be many stages of growth. The children in the last three conflicts (#19, #20, and #21) did at first shout at each other. Knowing how to problem-solve does not mean that children (or adults) will no longer get upset. Strong feelings are a normal, healthy part of life — they are not imperfections but rather the foundations for learning and living well. All of these children knew how to express strong feelings without physical hurting, and then moved forward to a solution — this is the great gift of problem solving. The three children in this last story did initially express strong feelings (*No! No! No!*), and they still moved quickly on to solutions. The non-hurtful expression and release of strong feelings, and the negotiation that followed, is what happened differently for Abby, Atticus, and the two boys.

Learning to problem-solve during conflicts is like learning a new language. Children, like adults, will have days they can access their best skills and days that they can't. Some become less emotional right away, while others may still yell at the beginning of a conflict. Each person, adult and child, will have an individual learning path with challenges along the way. But each will also have a day that he or she experiences how powerful and joyful it feels to succeed at solving a problem in cooperation with others. This life-long skill will benefit children and adults first as individuals, and then in turn they will inspire many others, changing the world around them.

# References


Copple, C., & Bredekamp, S. (2009) *Developmentally appropriate practice in early childhood programs* (3rd ed.). Washington, DC: NAEYC

Dowling, J. L., and Mitchell, T. C. (2007). *I Belong: Active learning for children with special needs.* Ypsilanti, MI: HighScope Press.

Evans, B. (2002). *You can't come to my birthday party! Conflict resolution with young children.* Ypsilanti, MI: HighScope Press.

Evans, B. (2007). *I know what's next! Preschool transitions without tears or turmoil.* Ypsilanti, MI: HighScope Press.

Faber, A., and Mazlish, E. (1999). *How to talk so kids will listen & listen so kids will talk* (20th ed.). New York: BackBay.

Gartrell, D. (1994). *A guidance approach to discipline.* Albany, NY: Delmar.

Kaiser, B., and Rasminsky, J. S. (2003). *Challenging behavior in young children.* Upper Saddle River, NJ: Pearson.


## Resources


Brazleton, T. B., and Greenspan, S. (2000). *The irreducible needs of children: What every child must have to grow, learn, and flourish.* Cambridge, MA: Perseus.

Carlsson-Paige, N., and Levin, D. E. (1998). *Before push comes to shove: Building conflict resolution skills with children.* St. Paul, MN: Redleaf Press.

Coles, R. (1997). *The moral intelligence of children.* New York: Random House.

Diffily D., and Morrison, K. (Eds.) (1996). *Family-friendly communication for early childhood programs.* Washington, DC: NAEYC.

Coloroso, B. (2004). *The bully, the bullied, and the bystander: From preschool to high school — How parents and teachers can help break the cycle of violence.* New York: Collins Living.

Dreikurs, R., and Cassel, P. (1991). *Discipline without tears: A reassuring and practical guide to teaching your child positive behavior.* New York: Penquin.

Epstein, A. S. (2009). *Me, you, and us: Social-emotional learning in preschool.* Ypsilanti, MI: HighScope Press.

Fried, S., and Fried, P. (1996). *Bullies and victims, Helping your child through the schoolyard battlefield.* Blue Ridge Summit, PA: M. Evans.

Gartrell, D. (2003). *The power of guidance: Teaching social-emotional skills in early childhood classrooms.* Florence, KY: Delmar Cengage.

Goleman, D. (2006). *Social intelligence: The new science of human relationships.* New York: Bantam.

Green, R. (1998). *The explosive child: A new approach for understanding and parenting easily frustrated, chronically inflexible children.* New York: HarperCollins.

Greenspan, S.I., & Salmon, J. (1995). *The challenging child: Understanding, raising, and enjoying the five "difficult" types of children.* Reading, MA: Addison Wesley Longman.

Jacobson, T. (2008). *"Don't get so upset!": Help young children manage their feelings by understanding your own.* St. Paul, MN: Redleaf Press.

Jensen, E. (2005). *Teaching with the brain in mind* (2nd ed.). Alexandria, VA: ASCD.

Katz, L. G., and McClellan, D. E. (1997). *Fostering children's social competence: The teacher's role.* Washington, DC: NAEYC

Pirtle, S., and Roerden, L. (1998). *Linking up! Using music, movement, and language arts to promote caring, cooperation and communication.* Cambridge, MA: Educators for Social Responsibility.

Rosenberg, M. B. (2005). *The surprising purpose of anger: Beyond anger management — Finding the gift.* Encinitas, CA: PuddleDancer Press

Whiting, B. B., and Edwards, C. P. (1988). *Children of different worlds: The formation of social behavior.* Cambridge, MA: Harvard University Press.

# Appendix

## Using Salt Timers

Large salt timers (see photo) can be very important tools for children during problem-solving and sharing. Parents and teachers might want to consider having at least one or more available at all times. They can be used for "showing" how much time is left before it's time to leave for school or how much time a turn will take with a toy or a swing. The person who is waiting gets to hold the salt timer, which is large and entertaining. Time is very obviously moving (versus a cooking timer with a dial which barely seems to move at all). Children can bang a big timer and actively shake it. Young children love them, so they are handy for siblings or mixed-age classrooms. The moving salt makes the movement of time visual and concrete.

When using a timer, whether at home or at school, keep the timer available and support children to negotiate how many times they will turn it over. The negotiation of the problem and of the number of turnovers is all part of the learning opportunity. Children sometimes begin by saying *I'll turn it over 10 times!* They love those big numbers! And they quickly learn the meaning of ten — it's too long! In time the negotiations will settle on numbers between one and four. Let children discover this on their own. This way there will be social and number learning all rolled together.

# About the Author

## Betsy Evans

Photo by Zoe Evans, age 5

**Betsy Evans** has been working in various roles in the early childhood field since 1974. She was a preschool program director and lead teacher for 23 years, and since 1989 has been a trainer, behavior consultant, and conflict resolution specialist. Betsy is the script author and co-producer of the videos *Supporting Children in Resolving Conflicts* (1998) and *It's Mine! Responding to Problems and Conflicts* (2003) and the author of *You Can't Come to My Birthday Party! Conflict Resolution With Young Children* (2002) and *I Know What's Next! Transitions Without Tears or Turmoil* (2007). She has presented trainings all across the United States, as well as in the United Kingdom, Ireland, Chile, Mexico, and Beirut, Lebanon. Having trained and observed in a wide variety of classrooms and settings, Betsy remains optimistic about the impact that young problem solvers will have, and are having, on families, schools, and communities: "Every child and every solution moves us all along the road to greater harmony and tenderness toward one another." Shown here with her granddaughter Sage, Betsy and Bunny made up a story of "One Watermelon Slice and Two Bunnies: What Can We Do?" Sage said, "Turns!"

## Jon Wilcox

**Jon Wilcox** is an illustrator and graphic designer. Originally from Detroit, he now resides in Seattle with his wife and their cat. In addition to working with HighScope, Jon has had the privilege of contributing to numerous education-oriented projects in the Midwest for institutions such as the Robert Crown Center for Health Education, the Economic Awareness Council, and the Chicago Children's Museum. Besides illustration and design, he also enjoys other creative pursuits such as making comics, screen printing, making music, and other things like riding his bicycle and reading books. Although Jon has no children of his own, he has been witness to a few situations where the information in this book would have proved very valuable, indeed!